BLOOM'S

HOW TO WRITE ABOUT

Langston Hughes

JAMES B. KELLEY

Introduction by Harold Bloom

BLOOM'S
LITERARY CRITICISM
An imprint of Infobase Publishing

Bloom's How to Write about Langston Hughes

Copyright © 2010 by Infobase Publishing
Introduction © 2010 by Harold Bloom

Bloom's Literary Criticism
An imprint of Infobase Publishing
132 West 31st Street
New York NY 10001

Library of Congress Cataloging-in-Publication Data

Kelley, James B.
  Bloom's how to write about Langston Hughes / by James B. Kelley ; introduction by Harold Bloom.
    p. cm. — (Bloom's how to write about literature)
  Includes bibliographical references and index.
  ISBN 978-1-60413-329-5 (hardcover)
  1. Hughes, Langston, 1902–1967—Criticism and interpretation. 2. Criticism—Authorship. I. Bloom, Harold. II. Title. III. Title: How to write about Langston Hughes. III. Series.

  PS3515.U274Z667 2009
  818'.5209—dc22
                    2009019583

Bloom's Literary Criticism books are available at special discounts when purchased in bulk quantities for businesses, associations, institutions, or sales promotions. Please call our Special Sales Department in New York at (212) 967-8800 or (800) 322-8755.

You can find Bloom's Literary Criticism on the World Wide Web
at http://www.chelseahouse.com

Text design by Annie O'Donnell
Cover design by Ben Peterson

Printed in the United States of America

MP MSRF 10 9 8 7 6 5 4 3 2 1

This book is printed on acid-free paper.

CONTENTS

Series Introduction   v

Volume Introduction   vii

How to Write a Good Essay   1

How to Write about Langston Hughes   51

   "The Negro Speaks of Rivers"   82

   "The Weary Blues"   94

   "I, Too"   101

   "Song for a Dark Girl"   107

   "Goodbye Christ"   115

   "Ballad of Booker T."   120

   "The Negro Artist and the Racial Mountain"   126

   The Big Sea   134

   "The Blues I'm Playing"   142

   "Father and Son"   152

   "Slave on the Block"   162

   Not Without Laughter   168

   Tambourines to Glory   179

Index   192

SERIES
INTRODUCTION

B LOOM's How to Write about Literature series is designed to inspire students to write fine essays on great writers and their works. Each volume in the series begins with an introduction by Harold Bloom, meditating on the challenges and rewards of writing about the volume's subject author. The first chapter then provides detailed instructions on how to write a good essay, including how to find a thesis; how to develop an outline; how to write a good introduction, body text, and conclusion; how to cite sources; and more. The second chapter provides a brief overview of the issues involved in writing about the subject author and then a number of suggestions for paper topics, with accompanying strategies for addressing each topic. Succeeding chapters cover the author's major works.

The paper topics suggested within this book are open-ended, and the brief strategies provided are designed to give students a push forward in the writing process rather than a road map to success. The aim of the book is to pose questions, not answer them. Many different kinds of papers could result from each topic. As always, the success of each paper will depend completely on the writer's skill and imagination.

HOW TO
WRITE ABOUT
LANGSTON HUGHES:
INTRODUCTION

by Harold Bloom

I T IS difficult to write well about Langston Hughes, since his tends to be a poetry that resists analysis. Popular verse, whether written by Carl Sandburg, who influenced Hughes, or Hughes himself, has to risk a kind of literal simplicity in order to reach and move its audience. Since all poetry depends on metaphor, and Hughes's images tend to be few and traditional, the expositor is left with little to employ as commentary.

One useful stratagem is to consult the copious histories of the Harlem Renaissance, of which Hughes was an ornament. Another is to read parts of his two autobiographies, which are alive and intensely aware.

What seems to me most vital and helpful is to explore Hughes's relationship to the blues and the high American art of jazz that burgeoned out of it. I recommend particularly the books on early jazz of Albert Murray, Gunther Schuller, and Marshall Stearns.

Hughes had imaginative powers larger than he could place in his work, because his sense of responsibility to his audience partly inhibited him. Nevertheless, his endeavor was a heroic one.

HOW TO WRITE
A GOOD ESSAY

By Laurie A. Sterling and James B. Kelley

WHILE THERE are many ways to write about literature, most assignments for high school and college English classes call for analytical papers. In these assignments, you are presenting your interpretation of a text to your reader. Your objective is to interpret the text's meaning in order to enhance your reader's understanding and enjoyment of the work. Without exception, strong papers about the meaning of a literary work are built upon a careful, close reading of the text or texts. Careful, analytical reading should always be the first step in your writing process. This volume provides models of such close, analytical reading, and these should help you develop your own skills as a reader and as a writer.

As the examples throughout this book demonstrate, attentive reading entails thinking about and evaluating the formal (textual) aspects of the author's works: theme, character, form, and language. In addition, when writing about a work, many readers choose to move beyond the text itself to consider the work's cultural context. In these instances, writers might explore the historical circumstances of the time period in which the work was written. Alternatively, they might examine the philosophies and ideas that a work addresses. Even in cases where writers explore a work's cultural context, though, papers must still address the more formal aspects of the work itself. A good interpretative essay that evaluates Charles Dickens's use of the philosophy of utilitarianism in his novel *Hard Times*, for example, cannot adequately address the author's treatment of the philosophy without firmly grounding this discussion in the book itself. In other words, any analytical paper about a text, even one that seeks to evaluate the work's cultural context, must also have a firm handle on the work's themes, characters, and language. You must look for and evaluate these aspects of a work, then, as you read a text and as you prepare to write about it.

WRITING ABOUT THEMES

Literary themes are more than just topics or subjects treated in a work; they are attitudes or points about these topics that often structure other elements in a work. Writing about theme therefore requires that you not just identify a topic that a literary work addresses but also discuss what that work says about that topic. For example, if you were writing about the culture of the American South in William Faulkner's famous story "A Rose for Emily," you would need to discuss what Faulkner says, argues, or implies about that culture and its passing.

When you prepare to write about thematic concerns in a work of literature, you will probably discover that, like most works of literature, your text touches upon other themes in addition to its central theme. These secondary themes also provide rich ground for paper topics. A thematic paper on "A Rose for Emily" might consider gender or race in the story. While neither of these could be said to be the central theme of the story, they are clearly related to the passing of the "old South" and could provide plenty of good material for papers.

As you prepare to write about themes in literature, you might find a number of strategies helpful. After you identify a theme or themes in the story, you should begin by evaluating how other elements of the story—such as character, point of view, imagery, and symbolism—help develop the theme. You might ask yourself what your own responses are to the author's treatment of the subject matter. Do not neglect the obvious, either: What expectations does the title set up? How does the title help develop thematic concerns? Clearly, the title "A Rose for Emily" says something about the narrator's attitude toward the title character, Emily Grierson, and all she represents.

WRITING ABOUT CHARACTER

Generally, characters are essential components of fiction and drama. (This is not always the case, though; Ray Bradbury's "August 2026: There Will Come Soft Rains" is technically a story without characters, at least any human characters.) Often, you can discuss character in poetry, as in T. S. Eliot's "The Love Song of J. Alfred Prufrock" or Robert Browning's "My Last Duchess." Many writers find that analyzing character is one of the most interesting and engaging ways to work with a piece of literature and to shape a paper. After all, characters generally are human, and we all know something about being human and living in the world. While it is always important to remember that these figures are not real people but creations of the writer's imagination, it can be fruitful to begin evaluating them as you might evaluate a real person. Often you can start with your own response to a character. Did you like or dislike the character? Did you sympathize with the character? Why or why not?

Keep in mind, though, that emotional responses like these are just starting places. To truly explore and evaluate literary characters, you need to return to the formal aspects of the text and evaluate how the author has drawn these characters. The 20th-century writer E. M. Forster coined the terms *flat* characters and *round* characters. Flat characters are static, one-dimensional characters that frequently represent a particular concept or idea. In contrast, round characters are fully drawn and much more realistic characters that frequently change and develop over the course of a work. Are the characters you are studying flat or round? What elements of the characters lead you to this conclusion? Why might the author have drawn characters like this? How does their development affect the meaning of the work? Similarly, you should explore the techniques the author uses to develop characters. Do we hear a character's own words, or do we hear only other characters' assessments of him or her? Or, does the author use an omniscient or limited omniscient narrator to allow us access to the workings of the characters' minds? If so, how does that help develop the characterization? Often you can even evaluate the narrator as a character. How trustworthy are the opinions and assessments of the narrator? You should also think about characters' names. Do they mean anything? If you encounter a hero named Sophia or Sophie, you should probably think about her wisdom (or lack thereof), since *sophia* means "wisdom" in Greek. Similarly, since the name Sylvia is derived from the word *sylvan,* meaning "of the wood," you might want to evaluate that character's relationship with nature. Once again, you might look to the title of the work. Does Herman Melville's "Bartleby, the Scrivener" signal anything about Bartleby himself? Is Bartleby adequately defined by his job as scrivener? Is this part of Melville's point? Pursuing questions such as these can help you develop thorough papers about characters from psychological, sociological, or more formalistic perspectives.

WRITING ABOUT FORM AND GENRE

Genre, a word derived from French, means "type" or "class." Literary genres are distinctive classes or categories of literary composition. On the most general level, literary works can be divided into the genres of drama, poetry, fiction, and essays, yet within those genres there are classifications that are also referred to as genres. Tragedy and comedy, for example, are genres of drama. Epic, lyric, and pastoral are genres of poetry. *Form*, on the other hand, generally refers to the shape or structure of a work. There are many clearly defined forms of poetry that follow specific patterns of meter, rhyme, and stanza. Sonnets, for example, are poems that follow a fixed form of 14 lines. Sonnets generally follow one of two basic sonnet forms, each with its own distinct rhyme scheme. Haiku is another example of poetic form, traditionally consisting of three unrhymed lines of five, seven, and five syllables.

While you might think that writing about form or genre might leave little room for argument, many of these forms and genres are very fluid. Remember that literature is evolving and ever changing, and so are its forms. As you study poetry, you may find that poets, especially more modern poets, play with traditional poetic forms, bringing about new effects. Similarly, dramatic tragedy was once quite narrowly defined, but over the centuries playwrights have broadened and challenged traditional definitions, changing the shape of tragedy. When Arthur Miller wrote *Death of a Salesman*, many critics challenged the idea that tragic drama could encompass a common man like Willy Loman.

Evaluating how a work of literature fits into or challenges the boundaries of its form or genre can provide you with fruitful avenues of investigation. You might find it helpful to ask why the work does or does not fit into traditional categories. Why might Miller have thought it fitting to write a tragedy of the common man? Similarly, you might compare the content or theme of a work with its form. How well do they work together? Many of Emily Dickinson's poems, for instance, follow the meter of traditional hymns. While some of her poems seem to express traditional religious doctrines, many seem to challenge or strain against traditional conceptions of God and theology. What is the effect, then, of her use of traditional hymn meter?

WRITING ABOUT LANGUAGE, SYMBOLS, AND IMAGERY

No matter what the genre, writers use words as their most basic tool. Language is the most fundamental building block of literature. It is essential that you pay careful attention to the author's language and word choice as you read, reread, and analyze a text. Imagery is language that appeals to the senses. Most commonly, imagery appeals to our sense of vision, creating a mental picture, but authors also use language that appeals to our other senses. Images can be literal or figurative. Literal images use sensory language to describe an actual thing. In the broadest terms, figurative language uses one thing to speak about something else. For example, if I call my boss a snake, I am not saying that he is literally a reptile. Instead, I am using figurative language to communicate my opinions about him. Since we think of snakes as sneaky, slimy, and sinister, I am using the concrete image of a snake to communicate these abstract opinions and impressions.

The two most common figures of speech are similes and metaphors. Both are comparisons between two apparently dissimilar things. Similes are explicit comparisons using the words *like* or *as*; metaphors are implicit comparisons. To return to the previous example, if I say, "My boss, Bob, was waiting for me when I showed up to work five minutes late today—the snake!" I have constructed a metaphor. Writing about his experiences fighting in World War I, Wilfred Owen begins his poem "Dulce et decorum est", with a string of similes: "Bent double, like old beggars under sacks, / Knock-kneed, coughing like hags, we cursed through sludge." Owen's goal was to undercut clichéd notions that war and dying in battle were glorious. Certainly, comparing soldiers to coughing hags and to beggars underscores his point.

"Fog," a short poem by Carl Sandburg, provides a clear example of a metaphor. Sandburg's poem reads:

The fog comes
on little cat feet.

It sits looking
over harbor and city
on silent haunches
and then moves on.

Notice how effectively Sandburg conveys surprising impressions of the fog by comparing two seemingly disparate things—the fog and a cat.

Symbols, by contrast, are things that stand for, or represent, other things. Often they represent something intangible, such as concepts or ideas. In everyday life we use and understand symbols easily. Babies at christenings and brides at weddings wear white to represent purity. Think, too, of a dollar bill. The paper itself has no value in and of itself. Instead, that paper bill is a symbol of something else, the precious metal in a nation's coffers. Symbols in literature work similarly. Authors use symbols to evoke more than a simple, straightforward, literal meaning. Characters, objects, and places can all function as symbols. Famous literary examples of symbols include Moby Dick, the white whale of Herman Melville's novel, and the scarlet *A* of Nathaniel Hawthorne's *The Scarlet Letter.* As both of these symbols suggest, a literary symbol cannot be adequately defined or explained by any one meaning. Hester Prynne's Puritan community clearly intends her scarlet *A* as a symbol of her adultery, but as the novel progresses, even her own community reads the letter as representing not just *adultery,* but *able, angel,* and a host of other meanings.

Writing about imagery and symbols requires close attention to the author's language. To prepare a paper on symbolism or imagery in a work, identify and trace the images and symbols and then try to draw some conclusions about how they function. Ask yourself how any symbols or images help contribute to the themes or meanings of the work. What connotations do they carry? How do they affect your reception of the work? Do they shed light on characters or settings? A strong paper on imagery or symbolism will thoroughly consider the use of figures in the text and will try to reach some conclusions about how or why the author uses them.

WRITING ABOUT HISTORY AND CONTEXT

As noted above, it is possible to write an analytical paper that also considers the work's context. After all, the text was not created in a vacuum. The author lived and wrote in a specific time period and in a specific cultural context and, like all of us, was shaped by that environment. Learning more about the historical and cultural circumstances that surround the author and the work can help illuminate a text and provide you with productive material for a paper. Remember, though, that when you write analytical papers, you should use the context to illuminate the text. Do not lose sight of your goal—to interpret the meaning of the literary work. Use historical or philosophical research as a tool to develop your textual evaluation.

Thoughtful readers often consider how history and culture affected the author's choice and treatment of his or her subject matter. Investigations into the history and context of a work could examine the work's relation to specific historical events, such as the Salem witch trials in 17th-century Massachusetts or the restoration of Charles II to the English throne in 1660. Bear in mind that historical context is not limited to politics and world events. While knowing about the Vietnam War is certainly helpful in interpreting much of Tim O'Brien's fiction, and some knowledge of the French Revolution clearly illuminates the dynamics of Charles Dickens's *A Tale of Two Cities*, historical context also entails the fabric of daily life. Examining a text in light of gender roles, race relations, class boundaries, or working conditions can give rise to thoughtful and compelling papers. Exploring the conditions of the working class in 19th-century England, for example, can provide a particularly effective avenue for writing about Dickens's *Hard Times*.

You can begin thinking about these issues by asking broad questions at first. What do you know about the time period and about the author? What does the editorial apparatus in your text tell you? These might be starting places. Similarly, when specific historical events or dynamics are particularly important to understanding a work but might be somewhat obscure to modern readers, textbooks usually provide notes to explain historical background. These are a good place to start. With this information, ask yourself how these historical facts and circumstances might have affected the author, the presentation of theme, and the presentation of character. How does knowing more about the work's specific historical context illuminate the work? To take a well-known example, understanding the complex attitudes toward slavery during the time Mark Twain wrote *Adventures of Huckleberry Finn* should help you begin to examine issues of race in the text. Additionally, you might compare these attitudes to those of the time in which the novel was set. How might this comparison affect your interpretation of a work written after the abolition of slavery but set before the Civil War?

WRITING ABOUT PHILOSOPHY AND IDEAS

Philosophical concerns are closely related to both historical context and thematic issues. Like historical investigation, philosophical research can provide a useful tool as you analyze a text. For example, an investigation into the working class in Dickens's England might lead you to a topic on the philosophical doctrine of utilitarianism in *Hard Times*. Many other works explore philosophies and ideas quite explicitly. Mary Shelley's famous novel *Frankenstein,* for example, explores John Locke's tabula rasa theory of human knowledge as she portrays the intellectual and emotional development of Victor Frankenstein's creature. As this example indicates, philosophical issues are somewhat more abstract than investigations of theme or historical context. Some other examples of philosophical issues include human free will, the formation of human identity, the nature of sin, or questions of ethics.

Writing about philosophy and ideas might require some outside research, but usually the notes or other material in your text will provide you with basic information, and often footnotes and bibliographies suggest places you can go to read further about the subject. If you have identified a philosophical theme that runs through a text, you might ask yourself how the author develops this theme. Look at character development and the interactions of characters, for example. Similarly, you might examine whether the narrative voice in a work of fiction addresses the philosophical concerns of the text.

WRITING COMPARISON AND CONTRAST ESSAYS

Finally, you might find that comparing and contrasting the works or techniques of an author provides a useful tool for literary analysis. A comparison and contrast essay might compare two characters or themes in a single work, or it might compare the author's treatment of a theme in two works. It might also contrast methods of character development or analyze an author's differing treatment of a philosophical concern in two works. Writing comparison and contrast essays, though, requires some special consideration. While they generally provide you with plenty of material to use, they also come with a built-in trap: the laundry list. These papers often become mere lists of connections between the works. As this chapter will discuss, a strong thesis must make an assertion that you want to prove or validate. A strong comparison/contrast thesis, then, needs to comment on the significance of the similarities and differences you observe. It is not enough merely to assert that the works contain similarities and differences. You might, for example, assert why the similarities and differences are important and explain how they illuminate the works' treatment of theme. Remember, too, that a thesis should not be a statement of the obvious. A comparison/contrast paper that focuses only on very obvious similarities or differences does little to illuminate the connections between the works. Often, an effective method of shaping a strong thesis and argument is to begin your paper by noting the similarities between the works but then to develop a thesis that asserts how these apparently similar elements are different. If, for example, you observe that Emily Dickinson wrote a number of poems about spiders, you might analyze how she uses spider imagery differently in two poems. Similarly, many scholars have noted that Hawthorne created many "mad scientist" characters, men who are so devoted to their science or their art that they lose perspective on all else. A good thesis comparing two of these characters—Aylmer of "The Birth-mark" and Dr. Rappaccini of "Rappaccini's Daughter," for example—might initially identify both characters as examples of Hawthorne's mad scientist type but then argue that their motivations for scientific experimentation differ. If you strive to analyze the similarities or differences, discuss significances, and move beyond the obvious, your paper should move beyond the laundry list trap.

PREPARING TO WRITE

Armed with a clear sense of your task—illuminating the text—and with an understanding of theme, character, language, history, and philosophy, you are ready to approach the writing process. Remember that good writing is grounded in good reading and that close reading takes time, attention, and more than one reading of your text. Read for comprehension first. As you go back and review the work, mark the text to chart the details of the work as well as your reactions. Highlight important passages, repeated words, and image patterns. "Converse" with the text through marginal notes. Mark turns in the plot, ask questions, and make observations about characters, themes, and language. If you are reading from a book that does not belong to you, keep a record of your reactions in a journal or notebook. If you have read a work of literature carefully, paying attention to both the text and the context of the work, you have a leg up on the writing process. Admittedly, at this point, your ideas are probably very broad and undefined, but you have taken an important first step toward writing a strong paper.

Your next step is to focus, to take a broad, perhaps fuzzy, topic and define it more clearly. Even a topic provided by your instructor will need to be focused appropriately. Remember that good writers make the topic their own. There are a number of strategies—often called "invention"—that you can use to develop your own focus. In one such strategy, called *freewriting*, you spend 10 minutes or so just writing about your topic without referring back to the text or your notes. Write whatever comes to mind; the important thing is that you just keep writing. Often this process allows you to develop fresh ideas or approaches to your subject matter. You could also try *brainstorming*: Write down your topic and then list all the related points or ideas you can think of. Include questions, comments, words, important passages or events, and anything else that comes to mind. Let one idea lead to another. In the related technique of *clustering*, or *mapping*, write your topic on a sheet of paper and write related ideas around it. Then list related subpoints under each of these main ideas. Many people then draw arrows to show connections between points. This technique helps you narrow your topic and can also help you organize your ideas. Similarly, asking journalistic questions—Who? What? Where? When? Why? and How?—can lead to ideas for topic development.

Thesis Statements

Once you have developed a focused topic, you can begin to think about your thesis statement or thesis, the main point or purpose of your paper. You must craft a strong thesis statement; otherwise, your paper will likely offer little more than random, disorganized observations about the text. Think of your thesis statement as a kind of road map for your paper. It tells your reader where you are going and how you are going to get there.

To craft a strong thesis statement, you must keep a number of things in mind. First, your paper's thesis should be a statement, an assertion about the text that you want to prove or validate. Beginning writers often formulate a question that they attempt to use as a thesis statement. For example, a writer exploring the presence of stereotypes in Langston Hughes's short story "Luani of the Jungles" might ask, What terms does the white man use to describe the black woman whom he says he loves, and which of these terms show his obsession with their racial differences? While asking a question such as this one is a good strategy to use in the invention process to help narrow your topic and find your thesis statement, this question cannot serve as the thesis statement because it does not tell your reader what you want to assert about the man's perspectives on racial difference. You might shape this question into a thesis statement by proposing a developed answer to the question that you just asked. You might write: Langston Hughes's short story "Luani of the Jungles" presents a relationship between a white man and a black woman that is ruined not by outside disapproval but rather by the man's own obsession with and oversimplification of their racial differences. The unnamed man in the story loses the love of his life and even drives himself to the point of insanity. Hughes's story ultimately illustrates a range of negative consequences that result from seeing others only in terms of racial stereotypes. Notice that this thesis statement provides an initial plan or structure for the rest of the paper. Notice, too, that the thesis statement does not necessarily have to fit into one sentence. After discussing the racial stereotypes contained in the terms that the man uses to describe his wife, you could examine the ways in which two worlds—one Western and white, the other African and black—are presented in the story and then explore the relevance of Hughes's story to an understanding of race relations in his time or ours.

Remember, too, that a good thesis statement makes an assertion that you need to support. In other words, a good thesis does not state the obvious. If you formulate a thesis statement about race and stereotypes by simply saying Racial difference is an important topic in "Luani of the Jungles," you have done nothing but state the obvious. Since Hughes's story is centered on the relationship between two characters, a white man and a black woman, there would be no point in spending three to five pages supporting that assertion. You might try to develop a thesis statement from that point by asking yourself further questions: How do the characters in Hughes's story talk about racial differences? Does the story seem to present a position for or against this way of talking about race? Does it matter that Hughes, because he was black, belonged to an oppressed and widely stereotyped racial minority in the United States? That he published the story in the 1920s in a largely segregated nation? Or that he had traveled to Africa before writing the story? Such a line of questioning might lead you to a more viable thesis statement, like the one in the preceding paragraph.

As the comparison with the road map suggests, your thesis statement should appear near the beginning of the paper. In relatively short papers (of three to six pages), the thesis statement almost always appears in the first paragraph. Some writers fall into the trap of saving their thesis statement for the end, trying to provide a surprise or a big moment of revelation, as if to say, "TA-DA! I've just proved that in 'Luani of the Jungles' Hughes uses the white man's all-consuming obsession with the black woman's skin and hair to show that stereotypes harm everyone, not just the person being stereotyped." Placing a thesis statement at the end of an essay can seriously limit the essay's effectiveness. If you fail to define your essay's point and purpose clearly at the beginning, your reader will find it difficult to follow your argument and understand the points that you are making. When your argument comes as a surprise at the end, you force your reader to reread your essay in order to assess its logic and effectiveness.

Finally, you should avoid using the first person ("I") as you present your thesis statement. Although writing in the first person is sometimes helpful, doing so gracefully is difficult. Beginning writers often fall into the trap of writing self-reflexive prose (writing *about* their paper *in* their paper). Often such writing leads to the most dreaded of opening lines: "In this paper I am going to discuss . . ." This self-reflexive voice makes for awkward prose and allows writers to boldly announce a topic while completely avoiding a thesis statement. An example might be a paper that begins as follows: "Luani of the Jungles," one of Langston Hughes's least-known but nonetheless interesting short stories, takes place on a ship sailing along the coast of West Africa, with a white male passenger giving an account of his doomed marriage to a black woman to one of the ship's crew members. In this paper, I am going to analyze what that man says. The author of this paper has done little more than announce a very general topic for the paper (the content of the man's story). While the last sentence might appear to be a thesis statement, the writer fails to present a purpose or an opinion about the significance of the man's story. To improve this thesis statement, the writer needs to back up a couple of steps. First, the announced topic of the paper is too broad; it largely summarizes the content of the story without saying anything about the ideas in the story. The writer needs to highlight what she considers to be the meaning of the story: What is the story about? The writer might conclude that the way in which the white man speaks about the black woman shows that he is not in love with her as a person but rather is obsessed with her blackness. From here, the author could examine the means by which Hughes's story communicates these and related ideas and then begin to craft a more specific thesis statement. For example, a writer who chooses to argue that this neglected short story by Hughes deserves more attention than it has received might craft, probably after going through several drafts, a thesis statement that reads: "Luani of the Jungles" deserves more attention for a number of reasons. For one, the story dramatizes the psychological cost to an individual who is obsessed with racial differences. Also, the story has much in common with more famous literary works, such as Joseph Conrad's *Heart of Darkness*, that feature white travelers to the Dark Continent. Finally, the story's narrator has clear biographical parallels to Hughes himself. Taking these three factors into account, the reader may come to see Hughes's story as both a criticism of racist stereotypes and an exploration of the author's own fascinations and disappointments stemming from his earlier travels to Africa as a young man.

Outlines

While developing a strong, thoughtful thesis statement early in your writing process should help focus your paper, outlining provides a tool for logically shaping that paper. A good outline helps you see and develop the relationships among the points in your argument and assures you that your paper flows logically and coherently. Outlining not only helps place your points in a logical order but also helps you organize the supporting points, weed out irrelevant points, and decide if necessary points are missing from your argument. Most of us are familiar with formal outlines that use numerical and letter designations for each point. However, the formal outline is not the only type of outline; you may find that an informal outline is a more useful tool for you. What is important, though, is that you spend the time to develop some sort of outline, whether it be informal or formal. This section of the chapter presents a series of informal and formal outlines that, taken together, demonstrate how outlines—like thesis statements—can be revisited and revised any number of times in the writing process to help the writer develop an increasingly sound and detailed framework for an essay. An essay that was developed through this series of outlines appears at the end of this chapter.

Remember that an outline is a tool to help you shape and write a strong paper. If you do not spend sufficient time planning your supporting points and shaping the arrangement of those points, you will most likely construct a vague, unfocused outline that provides little help, if any, with the writing of the paper. Consider the following example:

Thesis: Langston Hughes's short story "Luani of the Jungles" presents a relationship between a white man and a black woman that is ruined not by outside disapproval but rather by the man's own obsession with and oversimplification of their racial differences. The unnamed man in the story loses the love of his life and even drives himself to the point of insanity. Hughes's story ultimately illustrates a range of negative consequences that result from seeing others only in terms of racial stereotypes.

I. Introduction and thesis

II. Unnamed white man (husband)
    A. Appearance
    B. Reasons for being on the boat
    C. What he thinks of her

```
III. Black woman (wife)
     A. Name: Luani
     B. Appearance
     C. Reasons for not joining him on the boat
     D. What she thinks of him

  IV. Racist stereotypes

   V. Conclusion
     A. The unnamed man's obsessions with racial
        stereotypes destroy both his marriage and
        his mind
```

This outline has a number of flaws. First, the major topics labeled with the Roman numerals are not presented in a logical order. If the paper's aim is to show how the man's stereotyping ends the relationship and drives him to insanity, the body of the outline should first present the section showing that the man indeed engages in stereotyping. The outline gives this as topic IV; it probably should be topic II. The writer needs to establish this point convincingly before moving on. (The author also needs to decide on one term to use—*racial stereotypes* or *racist stereotypes*—and be consistent in using that term in both the thesis and the outline.) This section on stereotypes should probably be followed by a section that lists subtopics helping to show that these thoughts or behaviors on the man's part lead to the end of the relationship and the loss of his sanity. Similarly, the thesis makes no reference to a sustained discussion of both husband and wife, but the writer includes each as a major section of the outline. As the counterpart to the unnamed white man, the black woman may well have a place in this paper, but the thesis statement fails to provide details about her place in the argument that is being developed. Moreover, even if the sections on both the husband and wife are kept in the outline in their current form, they are not meaningfully balanced. The writer includes in section III, item A the phrase "Name: Luani"; this entry probably does not belong in the list of subtopics unless the name has a special meaning that will be discussed. Another problem is the inclusion of a single subsection in section V. An outline should not include an A without a B, a 1 without a 2, and so forth. The final problem with this outline is the overall lack of detail. None of the sections provides much information about the content of the argument, and the conclusion merely restates the thesis. It seems likely that the writer has not given sufficient thought to the content of the paper.

A better start to this outline might be the following:

Thesis: Langston Hughes's short story "Luani of the Jungles" presents a relationship between a white man and a black woman that is ruined not by outside disapproval but rather by the man's own obsession with and over-simplification of their racial differences. The unnamed man in the story loses the love of his life and even drives himself to the point of insanity. Hughes's story ultimately illustrates a range of negative consequences that result from seeing others only in terms of racist stereotypes.

I. Introduction and thesis

II. Man's stereotypes when talking about woman

III. Man's inability to bridge cultures, make real connections while staying with woman and her tribe in Africa

IV. Man's condition at the story's end

V. Conclusion

This new outline will prove much more helpful when it comes time to write the paper.

An outline like this can be shaped into an even more useful tool if the writer fleshes out the argument by providing specific examples from the text to support each point. Once you have listed your main point and your supporting ideas, flesh out the outline by listing supporting ideas and material under each of the main headings. From there, arrange the material in subsections and order the material logically.

For example, you might begin with the thesis statement cited above: Langston Hughes's short story "Luani of the Jungles" presents a relationship between a white man and a black woman that is ruined not by outside disapproval but rather by the man's own obsession with and over-simplification of their racial differences. The unnamed man in the story loses the love of his life and even drives himself to the point of insanity. Hughes's story ultimately illustrates a range of negative consequences that result from seeing others only in terms of racist stereotypes.   As noted above, this thesis statement already gives you the beginning of an organization: Start by demonstrating convincingly that the man indeed engages in stereotyping and then go on to show that his thoughts and behaviors drive a wedge between his wife and him, leading to the end of the relationship and the loss of his sanity. You might begin your outline, then, with the three body sections given in the previous outline: (1) the white man's use of stereotypes when talking about the black woman, (2) the man's inability to bridge cultures and make real human connections with the woman and her tribe in Africa, and (3) the man's condition at the end of the story. Under each of these headings you can list ideas that develop or support that particular point. Include references to sections of the text that help build your case. As you develop the outline, you may find that one section or another can be expanded with more items. In the outline presented below, the section about stereotypes has been expanded to include not just the man's stereotypes about the woman but also the narrator's stereotypes about Africa as a whole:

Thesis: Langston Hughes's short story "Luani of the Jungles" presents a relationship between a white man and a black woman that is ruined not by outside disapproval but rather by the man's own obsession with and oversimplification of their racial differences. The unnamed man in the story loses the love of his life and even drives himself to the point of insanity. Hughes's story ultimately illustrates a range of negative consequences that result from seeing others only in terms of racist stereotypes.

1. Introduction and thesis

2. Racist stereotypes
   - Stereotypes about the black woman, contrasted with the white man
     - Woman: "her dark body against my white one . . . its mass of bushy hair tangled and wild. . . . all the lure of the jungle countries" (422), "the ebony goddess . . . the dark princess who saved me from the corrupt tangle of white civilization" (422), "a delicate statue carved in ebony . . . a woman to write poems about, a woman to go mad over" (424)
     - Man: "strange, weak-looking little white man" (419), "beautiful brown-black people whose perfect bodies glistened in the sunlight, bodies that shamed me and the weakness under my European clothing" (423)
   - Stereotypes about black Africa, contrasted with white Europe
     - Paris: the "city of light and joy" (433)
     - Africa: dark, remote, and joyless: "a dense, sullen jungle" (420), a "colorless and forbidding country" (420), "the jungles hidden in the distant darkness of the coast" (421), "a shadow on the horizon" (425)

3. Man's passivity, inability to bridge cultures, inability to make real connections while staying with woman and her tribe in Africa
   - No effort to learn tribal language or customs

- No effort to communicate his concerns to her
- Connections between his passivity and his stereotyping (black is strong, virile; white is weak, impotent)

4. Man's condition at the story's end
- Literal condition
  - Nervousness
  - Restlessness
- Figurative condition
  - Trapped: this is his fourth time returning to the woman only to try to leave her again, every time taking a long journey by boat
  - Ambivalent: simultaneously attracted to and repulsed by the image of her that he has created in his mind; "I'm like a madman and she's like the soul of her jungles, quiet and terrible, beautiful and dangerous, fascinating and death-like" (425)

5. Conclusion

You would set about writing a formal outline with a similar process, though in the final stages you would label the headings differently. A formal outline for a paper that expands the thesis statement about "Luani of the Jungles" cited above—that the unnamed white man's obsessions with racial difference ultimately destroy his relationship with the black woman and drive him to madness—might look like this:

Thesis: Langston Hughes's neglected short story "Luani of the Jungles" deserves more attention for a number of reasons. For one, it dramatizes the psychological cost to an individual who is obsessed with racial differences and racist stereotypes. Also, it has much in common with a famous literary work, Joseph Conrad's *Heart of Darkness*, that features white travelers to Africa and that cleverly critiques white fantasies about black people. Finally, and perhaps most interestingly, the narrator of "Luani of the Jungles," who has clear biographical parallels to Hughes himself, also exaggerates racial differences and perhaps even engages in racist stereotyping. Taking these three factors into account, the reader may come to see Hughes's story as a criticism of racist stereotypes even though it does not fully escape them and as a possible exploration of the author's own fascinations and disappointments stemming from his earlier travels to Africa as a young man.

I. Introduction
    A. Story has been neglected
    B. Story has "limitations as art" (Rampersad 139)
    C. Thesis

II. Obsessions with racial differences and racist stereotypes
    A. White man's obsessions with Luani's blackness and explicit contrast with his own whiteness
        1. "At once I was fascinated. She seemed to me the most beautiful thing I had ever seen—dark and wild, exotic and strange—accustomed as I had been to only pale white women. . . . She waltzed as no woman I have ever danced with before could waltz—her dark body close against my white one, her head on my shoulder, its mass of bushy hair tangled and wild, perfumed with a jungle scent. . . . She seemed all I had ever dreamed of; all the romance I'd ever found

in books; all the lure of the jungle countries; all the passions of the tropic soul." (421–22)

2. "You'll be the ebony goddess of my heart, the dark princess who saved me from the corrupt tangle of white civilization, who took me away from my books into life, who discovered for me the soul of your dark countries. You'll be the tropic flower of my heart." (422)

3. "Like a delicate statue carved in ebony, a dark halo about her head, she stood before me, beautiful and black like the very soul of the tropics, a woman to write poems about, a woman to go mad over." (424)

4. "Four times that has happened now. Four times I've left her and four times returned. . . . Luani humiliates me now—and fascinates me, tortures me and holds me. I love her. I hate her, too. I write poems about her and destroy them. I leave her and come back. I do not know why. I'm like a madman and she's like the soul of her jungles, quiet and terrible, beautiful and dangerous, fascinating and death-like. I'm leaving her again, but I know I'll come back. . . . I know I'll come back." (425)

B. Narrator's obsession with Africa's blackness and implicit contrast with Europe's whiteness

1. Paris: the "city of light and joy" (433)

2. Africa: dark, remote, and joyless: "a dense, sullen jungle" (420), a

"colorless and forbidding country"
(420), "the jungles hidden in the
distant darkness of the coast" (421),
"a shadow on the horizon" (425),
nothing as colorful and as exotic
as what "one likes to imagine in the
tropics" (420)

C. Luani's emphasis on her own blackness and
her country's blackness

III. Parallels between "Luani" and *Heart of Darkness*

A. Africa is depicted as "an alluring,
destructive woman" (JanMohamed 90)

B. White man is "transformed by the
structure he sets in place" (JanMohamed
89) and "trapped by his own self-image"
(JanMohamed 90)

C. Frame narrative used in both stories

IV. Hughes's ambivalent and possibly racist views
of Africa

A. Parallels discussed in Rampersad's
biography

1. "African background" (139)

2. "crewmen on a steamer" (139)

B. Parallels not discussed in Rampersad's
biography

1. Poet

2. Mess duty on boat

3. Monkey

4. Disappointment that the reality of
Africa does not match what he has
encountered in books

V. Conclusion

A. How this neglected story can be read
meaningfully in multiple ways

   1. Critique of racist stereotypes
   2. Part of a broader literary tradition
   3. Reflection of Hughes's ambivalence toward Africa
  B. What the approach used in this paper illustrates more generally
   1. Value of revisiting neglected works
   2. Value of reading a literary work in more ways than one

As in the previous example outline, the thesis statement provides a solid foundation for the essay. A developed outline builds on that foundation and, in the end, provides an equally solid scaffolding for the actual construction (or writing) of the essay. In this formal outline, the writer is careful to arrange the supporting points in a logical manner and to show the relationships among the many ideas in the paper. An outline written at this level of detail may need to be revised several times during the drafting process of the actual essay; as a blueprint, the outline is a valuable planning tool, but even with the best of planning, small changes and adjustments will sometimes need to be made once the actual construction project has begun.

Body Paragraphs

Once your outline is complete, you can begin drafting your paper. Paragraphs are units of related sentences and are the building blocks of a good paper. As you draft the essay, you should keep in mind both the function and the qualities of good paragraphs. Paragraphs help you chart and control the shape and content of your essay, and they help the reader see your organization and your logic. You should begin a new paragraph whenever you move from one major point to another. In longer, more complex essays you might use a group of related paragraphs to support a single major point. In addition to being adequately developed, a good paragraph is both unified and coherent.

Unified Paragraphs

Each paragraph presents a single, clear idea or point. A unified paragraph carefully focuses on and develops this central idea without including extraneous ideas or tangents. For beginning writers, the most direct way to construct unified paragraphs is to include a topic sentence in each paragraph. This topic sentence should convey the main point of the paragraph, and every sentence in the paragraph should relate to that topic sentence. Any sentence that strays from the topic does not belong in the paragraph and needs to be revised or deleted. Consider the following paragraph about the meaningful similarities between Langston Hughes's short story "Luani of the Jungles" and Joseph Conrad's longer work *Heart of Darkness.* Notice how in the final three sentences, the paragraph veers away from the main point that the two stories have significant similarities:

> The connection made between the dark woman (Luani) and her Dark Continent (Africa) is one of several strong parallels between Hughes's story and Joseph Conrad's earlier and more widely read *Heart of Darkness,* a work that Hughes reportedly read the summer before his first trip to Africa (Rampersad 71). No fewer than three other parallels quickly emerge. For example, as Abdul R. JanMohamed has argued, Conrad "depicts the process whereby the colonist is transformed by the structure he sets in place" (89). Like the antihero Kurtz in Conrad's work, Hughes's stranger is "trapped by his own self-image" (90). Finally, both stories, by Conrad and Hughes, are part of a literary tradition of depicting Africa as "an alluring, destructive woman" (90). The man in Hughes's story speaks English and French, the two most commonly represented languages of the colonizing powers in Africa. Yet even as the man appears to be the one in control, he becomes powerless once he joins Luani in her homeland. Africa is entirely different from what he had hoped for: He is unable to participate in the unfamiliar rituals, cannot speak the local language, and is powerless to stop his wife from exercising her right to have multiple male lovers at one time.

Although the paragraph begins solidly and the first sentence provides the central idea of the paragraph, the author eventually goes off on a tangent.

If the purpose of the paragraph is to present a few meaningful parallels between the two stories, the sentences about the man's languages and his powerlessness in Africa are tangential. This material may fit better into a paragraph elsewhere in the paper, but it is out of place here. One strategy for revision is to delete these sentences from the paragraph. Another strategy is to consider if it is possible to revise the topic sentence of the paragraph and to strengthen the connections between these three final sentences and the rest of the paragraph.

Coherent Paragraphs

In addition to shaping unified paragraphs, you must also craft coherent paragraphs, paragraphs that develop their points logically with sentences that flow smoothly into one another. Coherence depends on the order of your ideas and sentences, but it is not strictly this order that is important to paragraph coherence. You also need to craft your prose to help the reader see the relationship among the sentences.

Consider the following paragraph about the parallels between "Luani of the Jungles" and *Heart of Darkness*. Notice how the writer uses the same ideas as the paragraph above yet fails to help the reader see the relationships among the points:

> The connection made between the dark woman (Luani) and her Dark Continent (Africa) is a strong parallel between Hughes's story and Joseph Conrad's earlier and more widely read *Heart of Darkness,* a work that Hughes reportedly read the summer before his first trip to Africa (Rampersad 71). As Abdul R. JanMohamed has argued, Conrad "depicts the process whereby the colonist is transformed by the structure he sets in place" (89). Like the anti-hero Kurtz in Conrad's work, Hughes's stranger is "trapped by his own self-image" (90). Both stories are part of a literary tradition of depicting Africa as "an alluring, destructive woman" (90).

This paragraph demonstrates that unity alone does not guarantee paragraph effectiveness. The argument is hard to follow because the author fails both to show connections between the sentences and to indicate how they work to support the overall point.

A number of techniques are available to aid paragraph coherence. Careful use of transitional words and phrases is essential. You can use transitional flags to introduce an example or an illustration (*for example, for instance*), to amplify a point or add another phase of the same idea (*additionally, furthermore, next, similarly, finally, then*), to indicate a conclusion or result (*therefore, as a result, thus, in other words*), to signal a contrast or a qualification (*on the other hand, nevertheless, despite this, on the contrary, still, however, conversely*), to signal a comparison (*likewise, in comparison, similarly*), or to indicate a movement in time (*afterward, earlier, eventually, finally, later, subsequently, until*). A few of these words and phrases can go a long way; a developed paragraph will often need only one, two, or three such transitional flags.

In addition to transitional flags, careful use of pronouns aids coherence and flow. If you are writing about *The Wizard of Oz,* you do not want to keep repeating the phrase *the witch* or the name *Dorothy.* Careful substitution of the pronoun *she* in these instances will aid coherence. A word of warning, though: When you substitute pronouns for proper names, be sure that your pronoun reference is clear. In a paragraph that discusses both Dorothy and the witch, substituting *she* for one of these characters will easily lead to confusion. Make sure that it is clear to whom the pronoun refers. Generally, the pronoun refers to the last proper noun that you have used. Confusion can also be prevented and coherence improved by consistently using a well-chosen noun after a demonstrative pronoun such as "this" or "that": Beginning a sentence with "This can be seen . . ." is ambiguous, whereas beginning a sentence with "This obsession can be seen . . ." is not. Do everything to make your subject clear and unambiguous.

While repeating the same name over and over again can lead to awkward, boring prose, repetition can help your paragraph's coherence. Careful repetition of important words or phrases will remind readers of your key points. It takes practice to use this technique effectively. You may find that reading your essay draft aloud can help you develop an ear for effective use of repetition.

For an example of how coherence can be improved, compare the paragraph above to the paragraph below. Notice how the author works with the same material but shapes it into a paragraph that is clearer and easier to follow:

> The connection made between the dark woman (Luani) and
> her Dark Continent (Africa) is one of several strong
> parallels between Hughes's story and Joseph Conrad's
> earlier and more widely read *Heart of Darkness*, a work
> that Hughes reportedly read the summer before his first
> trip to Africa (Rampersad 71). No fewer than three
> other parallels quickly emerge. For example, as Abdul
> R JanMohamed has argued, Conrad "depicts the process
> whereby the colonist is transformed by the structure
> he sets in place" (89). Like the anti-hero Kurtz in
> Conrad's work, Hughes's stranger is "trapped by his own
> self-image" (90). Finally, both stories, by Conrad and
> Hughes, are part of a literary tradition of depicting
> Africa as "an alluring, destructive woman" (90).

The topic sentence in this revised version of the paragraph includes the phrase "one of several strong parallels," which tells the reader to expect a discussion of more than one parallel between the stories. A subsequent, short sentence—"No fewer than three other parallels quickly emerge"— reminds the reader of the topic of this paragraph and tells the reader more precisely that three parallels remain to be discussed here. The first of these parallels is introduced with "For example," and the final parallel is introduced with "Finally."

Introductions

Introductions present particular challenges for writers. Generally, your introduction should do two things: capture your reader's attention and explain the main point of your essay. In other words, while your introduction should contain your thesis statement, it needs to do a bit more work than that. You are likely to find that starting that first paragraph is one of the most difficult parts of the paper. It is hard to face that blank page or screen, and as a result, many beginning writers, in desperation to start somewhere, begin with overly broad, general statements. While it is often a good strategy to start with more general subject matter and narrow your focus, do not begin with a sweeping statement such as "Everyone likes to be valued for who they are as an individual." Such sentences are nothing but empty filler. They help to fill the blank page, but they do nothing to advance your argument. Instead, you should try to gain your reader's interest. Some writers like to begin with a pertinent quotation or with a relevant question, and most open with an introduction of the topic they will discuss. If you are writing about Hughes's presentation of stereotypes in "Luani of the Jungles," for instance, you might think about beginning the paper by talking about how you would define important terms, such as "stereotype," in an interesting way. Give the author's full name and the full title of the text that you are writing about in your opening paragraph. Do not depend on your essay title to introduce the author and the text.

Compare the effectiveness of the following introductions:

1) Throughout history, people have been attracted to and frightened by people who are different from what they are used to, sometimes to the point of creating racist stereotypes that are harmful to everyone involved. Think of how you would feel if someone you loved valued you only for your skin color and not for your whole person. It would ruin the relationship between you and that person, wouldn't it? I feel that in this story, Hughes shows how a white man's obsession with a black woman's skin color does just that.

2) *Webster's Ninth New Collegiate Dictionary* defines stereotype as, among other things, "a standardized mental picture that is held in common by members of a group and that represents an oversimplified opinion, affective attitude, or uncritical judgment." This same dictionary also defines racism as "a belief that race is the primary determinant of human traits and capacities and that racial differences produce an inherent superiority of a particular race." What Langston Hughes presents in his story "Luani of the Jungles," then, we could call a set of racist stereotypes. In the mind of her white male lover, the African woman in this story is valued solely in terms of her racial difference and exotic features, particularly her thick hair and dark skin. The

man's view of the woman is certainly oversimplified and uncritical, and when he looks at her, he seems unable to see anything more than racial difference and unable to stop thinking about which might be superior, his whiteness and the Western world or her blackness and Africa. This is why we can say that he views her solely in terms of racist stereotypes.

The first introduction begins with a vague, overly broad sentence, gives undeveloped examples, uses "you" and "I" unnecessarily, and moves abruptly to the thesis statement without giving the full name of the author and the full title of the story to be analyzed. The introduction should clearly state what is under discussion and how the material will be discussed; it is not enough to give this information in the title of the essay. The second introduction works with the same material and thesis as the first, but it provides more detail and more thoughtful discussion, making this second introduction a much more interesting and successful opening to an essay. This second introduction defines two key terms, names the author and the story, gives some details about the content of the story, and most importantly ties everything together by repeating several key words and concepts from the definitions and relating those words and concepts to the story being analyzed. The thesis statement, found in the middle of the paragraph ("What Langston Hughes presents . . ."), gives the full name of the author and the full title of the work to be discussed. The paragraph ends with a restatement of the thesis. This second introduction is good, but it is not perfect and might be improved further. For example, the writer might revise the introduction to avoid the unnecessary use of "we" and might incorporate the knowledge that she has gained by looking up the definitions of the two words without quoting directly from the dictionary. As detailed in a later section in this chapter on avoiding plagiarism, "common knowledge" items, such as the general meaning of everyday words, do not need to be cited.

The paragraph below provides a third example of an opening strategy. This introductory paragraph begins by naming the author and the text that the essay will analyze and then moves on to introduce relevant information about the story in order to set up the essay's thesis:

"Luani of the Jungles" is not one of Langston Hughes's best-known short stories. It was published in 1926 but was not included in any of the numerous, subsequent collections of his stories. Hughes's biographer Arnold Rampersad writes that, even though the story might suffer from "limitations as art" (139), it marks Hughes's maturation as a writer. Irrespective of any artistic shortcomings, the story deserves more attention for a number of reasons. For one, the story dramatizes the psychological cost to an individual who is obsessed with racial differences. Also, the story has much in common with more widely read literary works, such as Joseph Conrad's *Heart of Darkness,* that feature white travelers to the Dark Continent. Finally, the story's narrator has clear biographical parallels to Hughes himself. Taking these three factors into account, the reader may come to see Hughes's story as both a general criticism of racist stereotypes and a more personal exploration of the author's own fascinations and disappointments stemming from his earlier travels to Africa as a young man.

Conclusions

Conclusions present another series of challenges for writers. No doubt you have heard the old adage about writing papers: "Tell us what you are going to say, say it, and then tell us what you've said." While this formula does not necessarily result in bad papers, it does not often result in good ones, either. It will almost certainly result in boring papers (especially boring conclusions). If you have done a good job establishing your points in the body of the paper, the reader already knows and understands your argument. There is no need to merely reiterate. Do not just summarize your main points in your conclusion. Such a boring and mechanical conclusion does nothing to advance your argument or interest your reader. Consider the following conclusion to the paper about the stereotyping of the African woman in "Luani of the Jungles":

In conclusion, Hughes presents a white Western man whose obsession with racial differences keeps him from finding peace. He is unable to live with his black

African wife, and at the same time he is unable to
leave her for good. Hughes, himself a black author,
must have been particularly strongly opposed to racist
stereotyping. As readers today, we certainly are, too.
Or at least I hope so.

Besides starting with a mechanical transitional device, this conclusion
does little more than touch on a few of the main points of the outline
(and it does not even touch on all of them). This conclusion is incomplete
and uninteresting (and maybe a little naïve).

Instead, your conclusion should add something to your paper. A good
tactic is to build on the points you have been arguing. Asking "why?" often
helps you draw further conclusions. For example, in the paper on "Luani
of the Jungles," you might explore why Hughes, based on what you know
of his biography and other writings, would present such a character as the
strange white man who is unable to move past racially connected stereotypes. Your conclusion could discuss whether the story presents Hughes's
criticism of racist views among whites or maybe even his own oversimplified views of Africa—or perhaps a combination of the two. Another
method for successfully concluding a paper is to speculate on other directions in which to take your topic by tying it into larger issues. You might do
this by envisioning your paper as just one section of a larger paper. Having
established your points in this paper, how would you build on this argument? Where would you go next? In the following conclusion to an essay
on "Luani of the Jungles," the author reiterates some of the main points of
the paper but does so in order to amplify the discussion of the story's central message and to connect it to the larger, more general topic of making
sense of literary works by using more than one method or approach:

This reading of "Luani of the Jungles" through several
approaches allows for a richer interpretation of
Hughes's story, moving past an initial uncovering of
racist stereotypes to a discussion of why Hughes, a very
talented and highly intelligent black author, might have
written such a story. In the final analysis, Hughes's
own ambivalence about the Dark Continent, stemming at
least in part from his 1923 boat trip to West Africa, may
be as much the source for this story as his desire to

criticize the widespread racist stereotypes, including highly eroticized stereotypes, of blacks by whites in the early 20th century. In a larger sense, too, this reading demonstrates the value both of reassessing a neglected short story and of approaching any literary work in more ways than one.

Citations and Formatting
Using Primary Sources
As the examples included in this chapter indicate, strong papers on literary texts incorporate quotations from the text in order to support their points. It is not enough for you to assert your interpretation without providing support or evidence from the text. Without well-chosen quotations to support your argument, in effect, you are saying to the reader, "Take my word for it." It is important to use quotations thoughtfully and selectively. Remember that the paper presents *your* argument, so choose quotations that support *your* assertions. Do not let the author's voice overwhelm your own. With that caution in mind, there are some guidelines that you should follow to ensure that you use quotations clearly and effectively.

Integrate Quotations:
Quotations should be integrated into your own prose. Do not just drop them into your paper without introduction or comment. Otherwise, it is unlikely that your reader will see their function. You can integrate textual support easily and clearly with identifying tags, short phrases that identify the speaker. For example:

> The narrator describes the husband as "a strange, weak-looking little white man."

While this tag appears before the quotation, you can also use tags after or in the middle of the quoted text, as the following examples demonstrate:

> "I'm trying to get away," the stranger admits to the narrator.

"I don't know why I destroy my poems," the stranger
says in the story. "But then there are many things I
don't know."

You can also use a colon to formally introduce a quotation:

The narrator seems disappointed that the real Africa
does not live up to his fantasies: "Nor were there
the brilliant jungle trees one likes to imagine in
the tropics. They were rather a monotonous gray-green
confusion of trunks and leaves. . . ."

When you quote brief sections of poems (three lines or fewer), use slash
marks to indicate the line breaks in the poem:

In the final lines of the poem, Hughes repeats the idea
that beauty and peace can be found in darkness: "Night
comes tenderly / Black like me."

Longer quotations (more than four lines of prose or three lines of
poetry) should be set off from the rest of your paper in a block quotation. Double-space before you begin the passage, indent 10 spaces
from the left margin, and double-space the passage itself. Because the
indentation already signals the inclusion of a quotation, you should
not place quotation marks around the quoted material inside a block
quotation.

The *Oxford Companion to English Literature* defines the
ballad as

a light, simple song of any kind, or a popular song,
often one attacking persons or institutions. . . .
In the relatively recent sense, now most widely
used, a ballad is taken to be a single, spirited
poem in short stanzas, in which some popular story
is graphically narrated.

Langston Hughes's poem "Ballad of the Landlord" includes
more than a few of the elements presented in this
definition.

A complete sentence followed by a colon is often used to introduce the
block quotation.

The opening stanza of "Ballad of the Landlord" sets up
a pattern that continues through most of the poem:

Landlord, landlord,
My roof has sprung a leak.
Don't you 'member I told you about it
Way last week?

This regular meter (alternating between four and three
stresses per line) and rhyme (with repeated sounds at
the end of the second and fourth lines of each stanza)
make this poem a ballad more than just in name.

As shown in the last two examples given above, you must interpret
the block quotations after you present them. Explain to the reader in
careful detail how each block quotation that you present helps advance
your argument at that point in your essay. You cannot assume that your
reader will interpret the quotations the same way that you do. In the
example given above that defines the word *ballad* and then moves on
to discuss "Ballad of the Landlord," you would want to give more than a
single sentence as your interpretation before moving on to a new point
in your essay. In fact, you could write a fully developed paragraph here,
drawing three or four key terms from the definition (for example, "light,
simple"; "attacking persons or institutions"; "spirited"; and "graphically
narrated") and discussing how these terms apply to Hughes's poem.
Similarly, in the example given above that includes the block quotation
of four lines from a poem, you might go on to demonstrate that English
and American folk ballads often use this same combination of meter and
rhyme in each stanza. As a general rule, it is good practice to write an
interpretation or explanation that is at least as long as the block quota-

tion itself and that makes explicit use of or reference to the material that is presented in the block quotation.

Quote Accurately

Anything within quotations marks must be the author's exact words. There are some rules to follow if you need to modify the quotation to fit into your prose.

1. Use brackets to indicate that changes have been made or material has been added to the author's exact wording. For example, you may need to add words or alter the grammar of the quotation to allow it to fit into your prose:

   > Because he loves Luani "[s]o much," the man claims, he "ha[s] no regrets on taking leave of [his] classmates nor upon saying adieux to the city of light and joy."

2. Use ellipses (three spaced periods) to indicate that words or phrases have been deleted from a quotation:

   > Still on the boat, the narrator is unimpressed by the closer view of the African coastline and seems to welcome the opportunity to move away from Africa and back out into the ocean: "the river gradually widened and we could smell the sea, but it was almost dinnertime before the ship began to roll slowly on the ocean's green and open waters . . . we were still very near the Nigerian coast, and the gray vines and dull trees of the delta region."

3. Use the ellipses after a period to delete a sentence or more:

   > The narrator describes the view of the African coastline from his boat with more than a hint of disappointment: "Soon we seemed to be floating through the heart of a dense, sullen jungle. . . .

```
Nor were there the brilliant jungle trees one
likes to imagine in the tropics."
```

4. Use a single line of spaced periods to indicate that you have omitted a line or more of poetry or one paragraph or more of prose:

```
Well, son, I'll tell you:
Life for me ain't been no crystal stair.
.  .  .  .  .  .  .  .  .  .  .  .  .  .  .  .
But all the time
I's been a-climbin' on.
```

Punctuate Properly

The punctuation of quotations often causes more trouble than it should. You will want to keep these simple rules in mind:

1. Periods and commas should be placed inside quotation marks, even if they are not part of the original quotation:

```
The narrator describes the husband as "a strange,
weak-looking little white man."
```

The only exception to this rule is when the quotation is followed by a parenthetical reference. In this case, the period or comma goes after the citation (more information on parenthetical citation appears later in this chapter):

```
The narrator describes the husband as "a strange,
weak-looking little white man" (419).
```

2. Other marks of punctuation—colons, semicolons, question marks, and exclamation points—should be placed outside the quotation marks unless they are part of the original quotation:

```
What is the effect of the repetition of the word
human in the second line of the poem "The Negro
Speaks of Rivers": "I've known rivers ancient as
```

the world and older than the flow of human blood
in human veins"?

The speaker in Hughes's poem "Ballad of the
Landlord" poses a series of defiant questions to
the property manager, including "Ten Bucks you
say I owe you? / Ten Bucks you say is due?"

Documenting Primary Sources

Unless you are instructed otherwise, you should provide sufficient information for your reader to locate the material that you quote. Generally, literature papers follow the rules set forth by the Modern Language Association (MLA). These rules can be found in the *MLA Handbook for Writers of Research Papers* (seventh edition). You should be able to find this book in the reference section of your library. Additionally, these rules for citing both primary and secondary sources are widely available from reputable online sources, such as the Online Writing Lab (OWL) at Purdue University. OWL's guide to MLA style is available at http://owl.english.purdue.edu/owl/resource/557/01/. The Modern Language Association also offers answers to frequently asked questions about MLA style on this helpful Web page: http://www.mla.org/style_faq. Generally, when you are citing from literary works in papers, you should keep a few guidelines in mind.

Parenthetical Citations:

MLA asks for parenthetical references in your text after quotations. When you are quoting prose (such as a passage from a short story, novel, or essay), include the page number or numbers in the parentheses after the quotation:

The white man's obsession with the black woman's racial
difference is clear from his first description of her:
"She seemed to me the most beautiful thing I had ever
seen—dark and wild, exotic and strange—accustomed as I
had been to only pale white women" (421).

When you are quoting poetry, include line numbers in the parentheses after the quotation:

> Hughes's speaker in the poem "I, Too" tells confidently of change that is bound to come: "I'll be at the table / When company comes" (lines 11-12).

Works Cited Page:

These parenthetical citations are linked to a separate works cited page at the end of the paper. The works cited page lists works alphabetically by the authors' last name. A basic entry for Hughes's short story "Luani of the Jungles" reads as follows:

> Hughes, Langston. "Luani of the Jungles." *The Collected Works of Langston Hughes*. Ed. R. Baxter Miller. Vol. 15. Columbia: University of Missouri Press, 2002. 419-25.

Additional information can be added to this entry, including the original publication date of the short story and the total number of volumes that make up *The Collected Works of Langston Hughes*:

> Hughes, Langston. "Luani of the Jungles." 1926. *The Collected Works of Langston Hughes*. Ed. R. Baxter Miller. Vol. 15. Columbia: University of Missouri Press, 2002. 419-25. 16 vols.

The *MLA Handbook* includes a full listing of sample entries, as do many of the online explanations of MLA style.

Documenting Secondary Sources

To ensure that your paper is built entirely on your own ideas and analysis, instructors often ask that you write interpretative papers using only the primary source or sources and not conducting any outside research. If you do conduct outside research, however, you must document any secondary sources that you use. You need to document direct quotations, summaries, and paraphrases of other people's ideas as well as factual information that is not common knowledge. Follow the guidelines above for quoting primary sources when you use direct quotations from secondary sources. Keep in mind that MLA style also includes specific guidelines for citing electronic sources. OWL's Web site provides a good summary: http://owl.english.purdue.edu/owl/resource/557/09/.

Parenthetical Citations:

As with the documentation of primary sources, as described in an earlier section of this chapter, MLA guidelines require in-text parenthetical citations of your secondary sources. Unlike the research papers that you might write for a history class, literary research papers following MLA style do not use footnotes as a means of citing sources. Instead, after a quotation, you should give the author's last name and the page number:

> "[W]hatever their limitations as art, the four stories that resulted steam suggestively of miscegenation, adultery, promiscuity, and the turmoil of sexual repression" (Rampersad 139).

If you include the name of the author in your sentence, then you would include only the page number in the parenthetical citation. For example:

> Arnold Rampersad writes that "whatever their limitations as art, the four stories that resulted steam suggestively of miscegenation, adultery, promiscuity, and the turmoil of sexual repression" (139).

If you are including more than one work by the same author, the parenthetical citation should include a shortened yet identifiable version of the title in order to indicate which of the author's works you are citing. If you are citing from a multivolume work by one author, as shown in the example, include the volume number:

> According to Arnold Rampersad, these stories have "limitations as art" (1: 139).

Similarly, and just as important, if you summarize or paraphrase a particular idea from your source, you must provide documentation:

While these stories do not belong among Langston Hughes's best works, they do signal his maturation as a writer because they address challenging and adult themes (Rampersad, 1: 139).

Works Cited Page:

Like the primary sources discussed above, the parenthetical references to secondary sources are keyed to a separate works cited page at the end of your paper. Here is an example of a works cited page. Note that when listing two or more works by the same author, you should alphabetize these sources by the first words in the title and, in all entries after the first for that author, use three hyphens followed by a period in place of the author's name. You can find a complete list of sample entries in the *MLA Handbook* or in a reputable online summary of MLA style.

WORKS CITED

Hughes, Langston. *The Big Sea*. 1940. *The Collected Works of Langston Hughes*. Ed. Joseph McLaren. Vol. 13. Columbia: University of Missouri Press, 2002. 16 vols.

———. "Luani of the Jungles." 1926. *The Collected Works of Langston Hughes*. Ed. R. Baxter Miller. Vol. 15. Columbia: University of Missouri Press, 2002. 419–25. 16 vols.

JanMohamed, Abdul R. "The Economy of Manichean Allegory: The Function of Racial Difference in Colonialist Literature." *"Race," Writing, and Difference*. Ed. Henry Louis Gates, Jr. Chicago: University of Chicago Press, 1985. 78–106.

Rampersad, Arnold. *The Life of Langston Hughes, Vol. 1: 1902–1941*. 2nd ed. New York: Oxford University Press, 2002.

Plagiarism

Failure to document carefully and thoroughly can leave you open to charges of stealing the ideas of others, which is known as plagiarism. Correctly and fully documenting one's sources is a very serious matter, and a plagiarized essay that is turned in for an assignment will probably result in a very poor grade and possibly other sanctions. To avoid plagiarism, place quotation marks around any language that you take directly from your source, even if you use just one or two words. For example, if you wrote, "These stories have limitations as art," you would be guilty of plagiarism, since you used Rampersad's distinct language without acknowledging him as the source. Instead, you should write: At least one critic has found that these stories have "limitations as art" (Rampersad 139). In this second example, you have properly credited Rampersad.

Similarly, you cannot omit a citation simply because you summarize the ideas of an author or change or omit a few words. Consider the following short passage from Arnold Rampersad's biography of Hughes and the three sample passages from student essays that use information taken from this passage. Rampersad's biography of Langston Hughes contains the following passage about "Luani of the Jungles" and a small set of other short stories written in 1926 that transform Hughes's West Africa boat trip into fiction:

> Under cover of the African dark, his ship of fiction plowed warmer, more sensual waters than he had ever sailed before; whatever their limitations as art, the four stories that resulted steam suggestively of miscegenation,. adultery, promiscuity, and the turmoil of sexual repression. . . . "Luani of the Jungles" is about the unhappy marriage of a white man, formerly a Sorbonne student, to a wealthy, educated Nigerian woman who promptly takes to the jungle once she returns to Africa with him. He must endure her hunting and fishing without him and then her taking the chief's virile son as a lover ("A woman can have two lovers and love them both," she states simply). Tortured ("she drives me mad"), the husband tries four times to leave her but always returns to Luani, even after she has a child by the chief's son. (139–40)

Below are two examples of plagiarized passages:

> "Luani of the Jungles" is one of Hughes's four short stories, all set in West Africa, that mark his growth

and maturation as a writer. These stories deal with more
challenging and adult themes than most of his earlier
work.

Hughes's story "Luani of the Jungles" has limitations
as art, but it is still important because, in writing
it, he ventured out into new waters. In "Luani of
the Jungles," the man attempts again and again to get
away from the woman, but he keeps coming back to her,
although she becomes pregnant by another man whom she
has taken as a lover (Rampersad 139).

While the first passage does not use Rampersad's exact language, it does
present the same idea that he proposes on the significance of "Luani
of the Jungles" without citing his work as the source for this material.
Because this interpretation is Rampersad's distinct idea, using Rampersad's material without giving him credit constitutes plagiarism. The
second passage has changed some wording and included a parenthetical
citation, but this paragraph, too, still is plagiarized. In this second passage, some of the same language ("limitations as art" is used word for
word), the same word order ("the husband tries four times to leave her"
becomes, through a series of word replacements, "the man attempts again
and again to get away from the woman"), and even the same controlling metaphor (a ship on the water) are taken directly from the original
passage in Rampersad's biography. The first plagiarized passage can be
fixed simply by adding a parenthetical citation. Because several elements
in the second plagiarized passage too closely echo the source material,
though, the revision here requires much more work: In addition to keeping the parenthetical citation, the author of this second passage needs
to place quotation marks around the borrowed words and rewrite the
rest of the passage entirely in her own words, style, and metaphors. As
these two examples illustrate, it is less work to avoid plagiarism from the
start than to have to check for it and correct it afterward. The following
passage represents an honestly and adequately documented use of the
original passage from Rampersad's biography of the writer:

Hughes's biographer Arnold Rampersad writes that,
even though "Luani of the Jungles" might suffer from

"limitations as art," it signals Hughes's maturation as a writer because he begins here to deal with more complex and challenging themes (139).

This passage acknowledges that the interpretation is derived from Rampersad and uses quotations correctly to indicate his precise language.

While it is not necessary to document well-known facts, often referred to as "common knowledge," any ideas or language that you take from someone else must be properly documented. Common knowledge generally includes the birth and death dates of authors, the publication dates of their works, and other well documented and widely distributed information about their lives and writings. A common guideline is that a certain piece of information is common knowledge if you can find that information in three print sources that present the information without citing sources. Despite this guideline, it is often difficult to know if the information that you uncover is common knowledge or not. Internet sources complicate matters even further, as Web authors frequently, perhaps even recklessly, copy and paste information from one website to the next with little attempt to document their sources. What looks like common knowledge on the Internet may actually be one person's original idea or research that has been copied again and again without giving due credit. When in doubt, document your sources.

Sample Essay

Ingrid Adamson-Smith
Mr. Zicarelli
English II
February 7, 2010

REEVALUATING THE RACIST STEREOTYPES
IN LANGSTON HUGHES'S "LUANI OF THE JUNGLES"

"Luani of the Jungles" is not one of Langston Hughes's best-known short stories. Written and published in 1926, the story was not included in any of the collections of stories that were published later in his lifetime. Nonetheless, Hughes's biographer Arnold Rampersad writes that, even though "Luani of the Jungles" might suffer from "limitations as art," it signals Hughes's maturation as a writer because in it he begins to deal with more complex and challenging themes (139). The story deserves more attention for a number of reasons. For one, it dramatizes the psychological cost to an individual who is obsessed with racial differences and racist stereotypes. Also, it has much in common with a well-known and widely read literary work, Joseph Conrad's *Heart of Darkness*, that features white travelers to Africa and that cleverly critiques white fantasies about black people. Finally, and perhaps most interestingly, the narrator of "Luani of the Jungles," who has clear biographical parallels to Hughes himself, also exaggerates racial differences and perhaps even engages in racist stereotyping. Taking these three factors into account, the reader may come to see Hughes's story as a criticism of racist stereotypes even though it does not fully escape them. The story can also be viewed as a possible exploration of the author's own fascinations and disappointments stemming from his earlier travels to Africa as a young man.

The main conflict in "Luani of the Jungles" is wholly internal. A white man, whom the narrator meets while working on a boat travelling the West Africa coastline, describes to the narrator his relationship with an African woman in terms that repeatedly draw on racist stereotypes. The image of Luani presented by this "strange, weak-looking little white man" (419) is oversimplified and uncritical; when he looks at her, he seems unable to see anything more than racial difference and unable to stop thinking about which might be superior, his whiteness and the Western world or her blackness and Africa. In the end, this man's descriptions of Luani and her people are racist because they are caught up in concerns of superiority and inferiority and because they deny the humanity and individuality of the woman and, by extension, of black Africans as a whole.

In talking to the narrator about his earliest impressions of Luani, the man shows his complete obsession with her racial difference:

> At once I was fascinated. She seemed to me the most beautiful thing I had ever seen—dark and wild, exotic and strange—accustomed as I had been to only pale white women. . . . She waltzed as no woman I have ever danced with before could waltz— her dark body close against my white one, her head on my shoulder, its mass of bushy hair tangled and wild, perfumed with a jungle scent. . . . She seemed all I had ever dreamed of; all the romance I'd ever found in books; all the lure of the jungle countries; all the passions of the tropic soul. (421-22)

As seen in this passage, the African woman has value to the man solely in terms of her racial difference and more exotic features, particularly her black skin and thick, untamed hair. He also demonstrates here his naïve, romanticized view of Africa as a place of "romance," "lure," and "passion"—a view that he says he has gained from reading books, including perhaps adventure stories such as H. Ryder Haggard's *King Solomon's Mines*.

The man continues to express this obsession with racial differences in what he says to the woman, as he reports it to the narrator of the story:

> You'll be the ebony goddess of my heart, the dark princess who saved me from the corrupt tangle of white civilization, who took me away from my books into life, who discovered for me the soul of your dark countries. You'll be the tropic flower of my heart. (422)

Again, he refers to his books but adds that they are merely a shadow of things compared to what she has to offer, which is "life" and an escape from his own "corrupt" culture. His statements may sound positive—after all, he seems to be valuing her culture over his—but they remain oversimplified, uncritical, and grounded in nothing more than his (and much of his culture's) imagination.

In a later point in the story, the man continues to think of Luani solely in terms of her racial difference: "Like a delicate statue carved in ebony, a dark halo about her head, she stood before me, beautiful and black like the very soul of the tropics, a woman to write poems about, a woman to go mad over" (424). Here, he continues to oversimplify matters and assign to her a whole set of values, at once good (such as "to write poems about") and bad (such as "to go mad over"). In using the word *statue* and the phrase *dark halo*, he goes so far in this passage as to transform her into a pagan idol that he must worship and perhaps even fear.

The man concludes this tale of idealization, even worship, with a surprising admission. He is trapped by his desire for Luani, and despite efforts to leave her and return to the "city of light and joy," whether that be Paris or some other Western city, he finds himself powerless to resist making the journey back to her over and over again. He remains caught up in his racist formulations of her beauty:

> Four times that has happened now. Four times I've left her and four times returned. . . . Luani humiliates me now—and fascinates me, tortures me and holds me. I love her. I hate her, too. I write poems about her and destroy them. I leave her and come back. I do not know why. I'm like a madman and she's like the soul of her jungles, quiet and terrible, beautiful and dangerous, fascinating and death-like. I'm leaving her again, but I know I'll come back. . . . I know I'll come back. (425)

Through the string of opposing terms that are used in this potentially startling admission—beginning with *left* and *returned*, *humiliates* and *fascinates*, *love* and *hate*, *write* and *destroy*, and *leave* and *come back*, but not ending there—he captures the essence of his oversimplified, even racist views on their differences. He can only see black and white in the most extreme manner, as wholly desirable or wholly detestable, as all good or all bad. He just cannot seem to decide for himself anymore whether one color or the other is all good or all bad.

Much like Luani, as she is represented through the man's eyes, the entire continent of Africa is depicted in the story as the embodiment of intense sensations of all sorts, of the idealized and the demonized—from romance, passion, and life to unchecked eroticism and even insanity. In this case, however, the racist stereotypes come mostly from the narrator and the structure of the short story; their effect is to present Africa as the opposite of civilized, enlightened Europe. Almost all of the action in the story takes place at night, and while in the story the city of Paris is referred to by the man as the "city of light and joy" (422), Africa is described consistently by the narrator as dark, remote, joyless, or foreboding; it is, for example, "a dense, sullen jungle" (420), a "colorless and forbidding country" (420), "the jungles hidden in the distant darkness of the coast" (421), and "a shadow on the horizon" (425). The narrator observes, with more than a hint of disappointment, that what he sees is nothing as colorful or as exotic as what "one likes to imagine in the tropics" (420). In short, almost every character in the story engages in stereotyping Africa. As reported by the man to the story's narrator, even Luani collapses the difference between her homeland and her own body: "You are coming with me back to my people," she says to him, "your whiteness coming to me and my dark land" (422).

The connection made between the dark woman (Luani) and her Dark Continent (Africa) is one of several strong parallels between Hughes's story and Joseph Conrad's earlier and more widely read work *Heart of Darkness,* a work that Hughes reportedly read the summer before his first trip to Africa (Rampersad 71). A comparison of the two works reveals a number of parallels. Abdul R. JanMohamed writes that Conrad's story is part of a broader tradition in Western literature of depicting Africa as "an alluring, destructive woman" (90). Hughes's story equally fits in this literary tradition. JanMohamed has also argued that in *Heart of Darkness* the initial distribution of power is reversed, and the white traveler to Africa—the "colonist," as JanMohamed calls him (89)—is "transformed by the structure he sets in place" (89) and "trapped by his own self-image" (90). Like the antihero Kurtz in Conrad's work, Hughes's white stranger is similarly transformed and trapped by his own oversimplifications and obsessions about racial difference.

The frame narrative, which allows Hughes to bury the white man's narrative within the black mess worker's story in "Luani of the Jungles," is a device potentially adopted directly from *Heart of Darkness.* As in *Heart of Darkness,* the frame narrative appears at the beginning and end and takes up a substantial part of the story. This frame narrative might allow Hughes to write about racist stereotypes that many white Westerners had or even still have about Africa, while distancing himself from those same stereotypes. Alternately, Hughes might be using the frame narrative to project his own naïve views of Africa onto a white man. The narrator is left uncertain as to the truth of the tale that he is told; he wonders if the strange man telling it "were crazy, or if he were lying" (425). The narrator sits "still in the darkness for a few moments, dazed" (425) at the story's end but quickly recovers and returns to the routines of life on the ship.

While it may not be good reading practice to assume that the narrator in a literary work is the same person as the author of that work, this particular story has clear biographical parallels. Rampersad suggests as much in his biography: "Luani" and a few related stories, he writes, are "set against an African background and involv[e] crewmen on a steamer called the *West Illana* but obviously modeled on the *West Hesseltine*, on which he had sailed to Africa" (139). Rampersad does not go on to explore these biographical parallels more specifically, but a review of the short story, the biography of Hughes, and Hughes's own novel-length autobiographical work, *The Big Sea*, reveals at least four clear parallels between the story's author and the story's narrator. The narrator is a poet, like Hughes. Like Hughes, too, he temporarily abandons his writing career to work on a boat sailing from New York to Lagos, Nigeria, and other places along the West African coast; purchases a monkey from an African trader (in all accounts, the monkey is red, wild, and prone to biting); and feels disappointed that Africa in reality does not live up to the exotic impressions and images that he had cultivated from reading books.

This reading of "Luani of the Jungles" through several approaches allows for a richer interpretation of Hughes's story, moving past an initial uncovering of racist stereotypes in the story to a brief examination of its parallels with Conrad's *Heart of Darkness* to a discussion of why Hughes, a talented and highly intelligent black author, might have written such a story. In the final analysis, Hughes's own ambivalence toward Africa, stemming at least in part from his boat trip in 1923, may be as much the source for this story as his desire to criticize the widespread racist stereotypes, including highly eroticized stereotypes, of blacks by whites in the early 20th century or to position his story within a larger literary tradition. In a broader sense, too, this reading demonstrates the value both of reassessing a neglected short story and of approaching any literary work in more ways than one.

WORKS CITED

Hughes, Langston. *The Big Sea*. 1940. *The Collected Works of Langston Hughes*. Ed. Joseph McLaren. Vol. 13. Columbia: University of Missouri Press, 2002. 16 vols.

——. "Luani of the Jungles." 1926. *The Collected Works of Langston Hughes*. Ed. R. Baxter Miller. Vol. 15. Columbia: U of Missouri P, 2002. 419–25. 16 vols.

JanMohamed, Abdul R. "The Economy of Manichean Allegory: The Function of Racial Difference in Colonialist Literature." *"Race," Writing, and Difference*. Ed. Henry Louis Gates, Jr. Chicago: U of Chicago P, 1985. 78–106.

Rampersad, Arnold. *The Life of Langston Hughes, Vol. 1: 1902–1941*. 2nd ed. New York: Oxford UP, 2002.

HOW TO
WRITE ABOUT
LANGSTON HUGHES

L ANGSTON HUGHES (1902–67) is easily one of the most significant modern American writers and perhaps the best-known and most widely taught African-American poet. When Hughes is mentioned, the first thing that may come to mind is the Harlem Renaissance, which was a blossoming of literature and other forms of artistic expression by and about blacks in the 1920s and early 1930s and was centered on Harlem in New York City, the "Mecca of the New Negro." The Harlem Renaissance is certainly important to understanding Hughes as a writer; after all, as Jean Wagner writes, "Langston Hughes was by far the most productive poet of the Harlem Renaissance" (386). However, he also continued to be productive and to remain widely read long after that period or movement had ended. To focus solely on Hughes as a poet of the Harlem Renaissance is to underestimate this writer's importance and relevance in the 20th century.

Hughes was one of the few artists and thinkers of the Harlem Renaissance to achieve lasting fame and recognition, and he lived through other important moments in American and African-American history. During the Red Scare of the early 1950s, for example, he was called before Senator Joseph McCarthy to testify (some might say apologize or even recant) concerning the left-leaning poetry that he had written in earlier years. To offer other examples of his lasting relevance, his later works can be understood in connection with the civil rights movement of the 1950s and 1960s as well as the emergence of black nationalism within the United States and the development of the idea of "negritude" in black populations around the world in the 1960s.

Just as Hughes was not simply a writer of the Harlem Renaissance, he was also not simply a poet. He is rightly known for his poetry, which was published in multiple volumes during his lifetime and which has secured him lasting fame. As the sixteen volumes of *The Collected Works of Langston Hughes* also demonstrate, he was the author of an enormous number of essays and short stories as well as several novels, plays, autobiographies, and other writings. In addition to keeping in mind that Hughes was more than a poet and more than a figure of the Harlem Renaissance, a writer may face several challenges when developing an essay about Hughes and his works, but none of these challenges should discourage the thoughtful reader and the careful writer.

One such challenge in writing about Hughes is presented by the apparent simplicity of many of his writings. Most of his poems and a number of his short stories are very short, use everyday language, and incorporate or imitate popular forms of culture—from the secular lyrics of blues and jazz to the patterns and phrases of African-American sermons—that are not traditionally considered typical or traditional material for serious literature. At least three critics have commented that Hughes's poetry has often been considered exempt from (perhaps even undeserving of) close, sustained analysis precisely because his poetry uses simple structures and is grounded in supposedly unsophisticated sources, including oral traditions and popular art forms. For example, Harold Bloom writes in the Editor's Note to *Langston Hughes: Comprehensive Research and Study Guide* that "Hughes' poems, populist and expressionistic, rarely demand, or receive, 'close reading.'" The critical statements on Hughes's works presented in that volume, Bloom continues, "tend, therefore, to deal with larger issues" (8). Similarly, Steven C. Tracy writes that "[i]t is almost as if Hughes' working with the oral traditions precluded for many scholars any close textual study of his written work" (2). Finally, Arnold Rampersad writes that many readers have found Hughes's poetry to be lacking in comparison to more purposefully complex works, such as the modernist poems of T.S. Eliot, and thus have judged it "far too simple to be admired" (Hughes, *The Collected Works of Langston Hughes* 1:4). To varying degrees, however, all three critics have demonstrated through their respective works that close textual analysis of Hughes's poetry is possible and that, when coupled with a discussion of larger and closely related issues, Hughes's work presents a wide range of opportunities for original reading, research, and writing.

A related challenge faced by someone writing about Hughes concerns form and intertextuality (the influence other writings have on an individual work). Hughes produced innovative texts in which he incorporates many elements from popular songs, sermons, and other forms of creative expression in African-American popular culture in the first half of the 20th century. If you ask yourself whether or not some of these individual pieces are indeed poems and whether or not a group of these poems might be better described as a collection of song lyrics sung by others, you certainly would not be alone. Hughes's contemporary Countee Cullen, who was also a poet of the Harlem Renaissance but who wrote in more conventional forms, asked this question more than once in published reviews of Hughes's second volume of poetry. Similarly, many years later, the poet Leroi Jones (or Amiri Baraka) pronounced in his review of *Tambourines to Glory* that Hughes was more a collector of folklore than he was a literary artist.

On a related note, Hughes published many poems and other works that feature similar themes, such as the imagined and real histories of African Americans or the complexities and tensions of black identity in the United States and beyond. If you decide to write about any of Hughes's works that include the theme of imagined and real histories of African Americans, for example, you will have to decide whether or not you will take into account his treatments of this same theme in works other than the one that you initially planned to focus on. In other words, you will want to determine whether you consider each individual poem to contain wholly separate and unique ideas or whether you see his poems as intimately connected to one another and thus find it is useful or even necessary, for example, to read "The Negro Speaks of Rivers" alongside "Negro" (originally entitled "Proem"). These two poems from Hughes's first volume of poetry both take the reader on much the same (perhaps partly imagined and partly real) journey across centuries and continents.

A final challenge presents itself in writing about Hughes's psychology and other personal subjects, particularly as they may be reflected in his most popular and most frequently anthologized poems of the 1920s. In many of his early works and in his life in general, Hughes made a sustained effort to present a more optimistic or joyful attitude to the public.

The public persona that he frequently presents and that is reinforced by the 1959 edition *Selected Poems* is similar in some ways to the public persona cultivated by Robert Frost in his poetry; the persona encourages readers simply to admire the sheer optimism of the speaker in many of his poems in place of attempting to understand the poet's true psychology. In Hughes's early and widely read poem "I, Too" (initially known as "Epilogue"), for example, the speaker clearly understands that he is living in a segregated world: "They send me to the kitchen to eat / When company comes" (lines 3–4), he notes matter-of-factly. Rather than reacting with righteous anger or impotent frustration, however, he continues to "laugh" and "eat well" and "grow strong" (lines 5–7). Change is bound to come, the speaker in the poem concludes, primarily not because his oppressors will come to fear his growing strength (although that, too, may be hinted at in the poem's use of the word *dare*) but rather because they will begin finally to appreciate his unique value as an individual: "They'll see how beautiful I am / And be ashamed" (lines 16–17). Similar optimism in the speaker can be seen in the life advice given in "Mother to Son," in the unequivocal praise of blackness as something beautiful in "Dream Variation," and in the short piece titled "Poem" that begins "The night is beautiful, / So the faces of my people" (lines 1–2). The true source of some of the best of Hughes's poetry may have been the opposite of this sheer optimism. In the essay "The Origins of Poetry in Langston Hughes," Arnold Rampersad has argued that these works were written in periods of his life when he was ill or unhappy.

Even with tremendous public recognition and years of living in the spotlight, Hughes remained a private person. Wallace Thurman, a good acquaintance of Hughes and a fellow artist of the Harlem Renaissance, writes in his highly satirical and largely autobiographical novel *Infants of the Spring* that the character modeled on Hughes "was the most close-mouthed and cagey individual [Thurman] had ever known when it came to personal matters" and concludes that Hughes "[e]ither . . . had no depth whatsoever, or else he was too deep for plumbing by ordinary mortals" (232). As a result, one of the greatest challenges in writing about the connection between Hughes's life and his literary works is to understand the poet himself through the work. Was Hughes gay, for example? His two main biographers, after reviewing many of the same details of his life carefully, have arrived at different conclusions. Was Hughes politically radical throughout his life or only for a while in the 1930s? Hughes was certainly more overtly political in the 1930s than he was at earlier and later moments in his career, but critics similarly disagree over the extent to which Hughes distanced himself from radical politics in the 1940s and later decades.

If you choose to write an essay on one or more of the connections between Hughes's writing and the events in his life or elements of his psychology, do not simply rely on what you think that you know about Hughes or find in simplistic summaries and overviews, such as in the results of a simple Internet search. Instead, you will need to review biographical and critical studies of the poet. You may start by scanning relevant sections of Faith Berry's and Arnold Rampersad's biographies. Use the tables of contents and indexes to locate more quickly the information that you are seeking about a specific title or topic or a specific period or event in Hughes's life. These biographies, as good as they are, are simply one set of resources among many, and the more reading you do of biographical and critical studies, the more you will be able to develop for yourself and for your essay a complex and supported understanding of the poet's life, psychology, and works.

For you to face these challenges in writing about Hughes, you will need both to perform your own careful, close readings of his works as well as to review some of what others have written about these subjects before you. Some mentors and writing manuals will advise you to do extensive background reading on the author's life and works before you begin to develop your own thoughts and draft your own essay. Such an approach works well for some writers, no doubt, but it can easily overwhelm the beginning writer and can even more easily interfere with the writer's personal exploration of the text or texts that she or he has chosen to analyze.

Instead of first reading other people's ideas and then making sense of how everything is connected, before beginning an initial draft of your own essay, you are encouraged to see thinking and writing as interconnected, not separate, processes. Read the primary material by Hughes first, and then begin to write about it from your own perspective. As you are writing, return every so often to the primary text or texts for another reading and pause every so often in your thinking and writing about Hughes to review a few published statements about the material that you are analyzing. Approach writing as a recursive process, a process of regularly circling back to the starting point in order to generate and incorporate new insights of your own and newly gained information from outside sources. Good writing—whether on Hughes or practically any other subject in literature—returns frequently to the text and creates ever-widening circles of understanding.

You are encouraged here to begin your writing about Hughes with your own understanding of the text. You need to be willing to revise your views, of course, as you reread the material that you have selected and as you locate and review secondary sources that present the life of the poet, the historical context, and the relevant published statements on the material that you are analyzing. Above all, you will also want to do your best to explain clearly to the reader the process of how you arrived at your own views. You cannot simply state that things are so; the reader will want to see argument and evidence, beginning with your thesis statement. Already in the first draft of your essay, as discussed in the opening chapter, you will want to present a thesis statement making an assertion that you will need to support in the body of the essay.

READING TO WRITE

Writing about Hughes effectively requires writing about one or more of his works effectively. To begin working on such an essay, you will want to narrow down your potential topic to a particular work or a set of related works, as it would be impossible to cover in a developed and detailed way all of Hughes's writings—poems, essays, plays, autobiographical writings, short stories, novels, and other works—in a single essay.

Consider the anticipated length of your essay, the number and length of the works that you are planning to analyze, and the number of outside sources that you might incorporate as you plan your paper. You will want to make certain that you have enough but not too much space in your essay to analyze the work or works that you have selected as well as enough time to complete the tasks that you have set for yourself.

If you are planning to analyze two or more works by Hughes, you will want to understand and express your rationale for selecting these texts and discussing them together in your essay. Sometimes your reasons for selecting two or more particular texts will be obvious. For example, you may choose two essays written in two different decades in Hughes's life in order to show his changing views on the responsibilities of the artist. At other times, however, you may be drawn to—and thus find yourself grouping—two or more works together for reasons that you cannot quite explain. In this case, you will need to make sense of your reasons so that the reader is not presented with what looks like a random and meaningless grouping. The reader will almost always want to see an explicit statement that explains your choice of texts.

A series of sample topics is presented in the final section of this chapter, and in the final sections of all chapters that follow, for you to consider when writing about Hughes and his works. Each sample topic is accompanied by a work or small group of works that you may choose to focus on, but these specific titles are merely suggestions. You may want to substitute another title or two for the ones associated with a particular topic suggestion. Whenever possible, you should choose material to work with that you find interesting and promising. Your topic should be suitably complex for the length of the essay that you are planning to write. A short paper may be little more than a close reading of a single poem, short story, or essay by Hughes, for example, while a long paper may require that you discuss two or more works and incorporate several published statements by critics. In any case, be certain that you fully understand the length and content requirements, if any, of the paper that you are preparing to write.

Once you have a general sense of your topic and have selected the particular work or works that you want to analyze in your essay, reread that material carefully. In this rereading of Hughes's writing, pay attention to any details that seem to relate to your topic and begin to identify particular passages that may deserve special attention in your essay. Keeping detailed notes as you read and reread is a good idea. Hughes's works can appear deceptively simple and often require several close readings. If the material that you are working with is relatively short, you may want to photocopy or print the material and work from the copy. Working from hard copy of an individual poem or a set of poems, for example, will allow you to notate directly the text that you are analyzing and will make a number of things much easier, including identifying repeated phrases or patterns or recording any questions or comments that may arise during your reading of the text.

TOPICS AND STRATEGIES
Themes

Literary themes are abstract ideas that are often but not always phrased as conflicts or combinations—such as "nature versus nurture" or "crime and punishment." These often complex notions help organize and unify a literary work. A single work can and often does have several themes, and a writer often addresses the same theme or set of themes across several works and perhaps even across an entire career. Hughes's writing, varied as it is, tends to engage a set of related central ideas and concerns. For example, in many of Hughes's works you may find the tension between artistic freedom and artistic responsibility. A successful essay on Hughes can examine the development of a particular theme within a single work or across several works.

Sample Topics:

1. **Black is beautiful:** Explore Hughes's celebration of blackness—or his celebration of a wide range of skin tone—in his poetry or other writings. You may choose, for example, to explore the possibility that Hughes, in this very celebration, prefigures the sensibility that is captured in the phrase "black is beautiful" and that is commonly associated with the 1960s and later.

   You may want to start with Hughes's essay "The Negro Artist and the Racial Mountain," which boldly states: "Why should I want to be white? I am a Negro—and beautiful!" (35). This theme continues in his poetry: Consider discussing, among others, the poems "Dream Variation" and "Harlem Sweeties." To get a better sense of how many African Americans have seen themselves as having to resist the dominant culture's standards of beauty, you may wish to read *The Autobiography of Malcolm X*, which discusses, among other things, the aesthetics and politics of skin color, hair styles, and racial identity. You may also consider how Hughes might have been ahead of his time in embracing the word *black*, a word that we may hear used frequently today but that was considered a less polite term than "Negro" or "brownskin" in the early decades of the 20th century. As Hughes writes in his autobiographical work of 1940, *The Big Sea*, "most dark Negroes in America do not like the word black at all. They prefer to be referred to as *brownskin* or at the most as *dark* brownskin—no matter how dark they really are" (96–97).

As is possible with many topics, you may want to complicate your approach and address also the less positive aspects of Hughes's attention to varying skin tones. His celebration of these varying skin tones may border on fetishization or primitivism, for example, and his description of women's skin tones in terms of edible objects, as seen in nearly every line of the poem "Harlem Sweeties," for example, may suggest a treatment of his subjects that is not particularly positive, respectful, or empowering. For a discussion of this topic of the less desirable ramifications of the concept "black is beautiful" in Hughes's short story "Luani of the Jungles," see the sample student essay that appears at the end of this volume's opening chapter.

2. **Race relations in the United States and abroad:** Explore Hughes's treatment of contemporary race relations in his poetry or prose. You may wish to focus on the treatment of blacks in particular or the treatment of racial and ethnic minorities in general.

The initial poem in Hughes's first published volume of poetry—now called "Negro" but originally published under the title "Proem"—establishes connections between the oppression of blacks in the United States in his time and the oppression of blacks around the world throughout time by discussing the two side by side. One such paired set of lines in the poem reads "Cæsar told me to keep his door-steps clean. / I brushed the boots of Washington" (lines 5–6). You may find yourself expanding your treatment of this topic to include a discussion of the parallels that Hughes establishes between the oppression of black people and the oppression of all peoples of color. For this topic, consider reviewing the well-known poem "Let America Be America Again" or his lesser-known poems, such as "Kids Who Die," "The English," and "Black Seed," among many others. Other materials for analysis in your essay might include Hughes's two essays on Haiti written in the early 1930s, "People Without Shoes" and "White Shadows in a Black Land," or his critiques of white European involvement in Africa in his autobiographical work *The Big Sea*.

3. **Artistic freedom and artistic responsibility:** Examine Hughes's views on the duties of the artist, particularly the black artist, and reflect on how these views are manifested in one or more specific works by Hughes.

   You may choose to focus on Hughes's essays such as "The Negro Artist and the Racial Mountain" and "To Negro Writers," where his position on the duties of the black artist is mostly clearly articulated. In your paper, you may be interested in exploring whether Hughes's view of these duties remains constant throughout his career or changes dramatically over time. Whenever possible, present and discuss specific examples of Hughes's works to support your main points.

Character

You may want to begin your process of writing about characters in one or more of Hughes's works by deciding on a particular category of people. You may look at how women characters are presented in one or more of his short stories, for example. If the category of women characters seems too large, you may narrow the scope of your inquiry to something more precise but not too limiting, such as women blues singers. The following sample topics encourage you to consider other such categories, the artist as character and the biracial character. A highly creative person, Hughes has much to say about creativity and even more to say about the related question of where the artist's responsibilities lie, whether to herself or her race. Or, as Hughes was raised in a family that did not embrace black culture and identity, you may choose to focus on the internal conflicts or struggles of the biracial characters who frequently appear in his writing. Whichever type of character you choose, you will want to reread the works that you plan to analyze, taking careful and detailed notes on these specific characters as you do, and then begin to analyze the characters in order to draw conclusions. Based on your study of one or more artist characters or biracial characters in his works, begin to construct an argument about Hughes's understanding of the duties of the black artist or of the challenges biracial persons faced in the first half of the 20th century. Your emotional response to a fictional creation—assessing a character's likeability—is a good place to start, but in the course of planning and drafting your paper, you will want to move past emotional responses and into analysis.

Sample Topics:

1. **Artists:** A number of Hughes's works deal explicitly or implicitly with the creative process of writers, musicians, or other artists. Examine one or more of his works dealing with this topic.

   You may choose to focus on essays such as "The Negro Artist and the Racial Mountain" and "To Negro Writers," a poem such as "The Weary Blues," and/or the short story "The Blues You Are Playing." As you read and reread these works, take note of what you learn about the artists and their work, paying particular attention to any possible connections between their race and their responsibilities as an artist or between their race and the expectations of their audiences and patrons. Begin to form your own generalizations about Hughes's view of the black artist based on your analysis of these works. You may ask, for example, whether Hughes sees the artist purely as a creative individual, for example, or as a creative individual who has responsibilities greater than those to herself and her art. Or you may wish to investigate whether Hughes's views of the artist are consistently or inconsistently articulated in one particular period of his life, remain largely consistent over the course of his life, or change significantly over time. Whatever your generalization, you will need to support your overall claim through a careful analysis of two or more specific texts.

2. **Biracial characters:** Focus on the internal and external struggles of one or more of the biracial characters who appear in Hughes's poetry or prose.

   Texts for this focus on biracial characters in Hughes's writings might include the poems "Cross," "Mulatto," "Red Silk Stockings," "Ruby Brown," and "Christ in Alabama"; the play *Mulatto*; the short story "Father and Son"; and perhaps even Hughes's account of his first trip to Africa, recorded in *The Big Sea*, in which he explains that the Africans he met said that he was dark but not black. Whichever biracial characters in Hughes's writing you decide to examine, be sure to learn everything that you can about them. In particular, examine their dialogue, behaviors, thoughts (to the extent that you have access to them), and relationships with other characters. You may ask yourself whether there is a pattern in Hughes's writing of biracial male characters with white fathers and black mothers, for example, or you may explore whether any of these characters succeed in resolving the struggles that they experience. You may want to conduct some research on the motif of the "tragic mulatta" or, as is more commonly seen in Hughes's writing, the "tragic mulatto." You may explore whether Hughes simply works within this longstanding tradition or adds to or revises the tradition in some way.

History and Context

Hughes's writing has a distinctly contemporary feel. Because his style and vocabulary come across as familiar to us, his work is nowhere as challenging for us to read as writers known as stylistic innovators or working in another time period. One drawback of this familiarity is that we may have a tendency to assume that his world was nearly identical to our own. While, admittedly, you cannot abandon your own assumptions and ideas when you read his work, you must understand the limitations of projecting these assumptions and ideas onto Hughes's writing. If you want to develop a fuller understanding of Hughes and his works, you need to improve your understanding of what was happening around him as he lived and wrote.

If you do not attempt to step outside a modern perspective, for example, you will fail to take into account the early-20th-century notions of racial identity and race relations, of gender roles and psychology, or of the United States' uneven commitment to realizing its ideals of inalienable human rights for all within its own borders and its dramatically changing relationship with the world at large. However, if you spend time doing some research, discovering what ideas held sway in the society of which Hughes was a member and what issues dominated the headlines of his time, for example, you are much more likely to pick up on nuances that you may otherwise miss and thus have a better chance of arriving at Hughes's position on various issues. Compulsory segregation and lynching are no longer realities affecting the lives of individuals in the present day, for example, as they were in the early 20th century, and the popular reactions to segregation and lynching then and now probably differ significantly, too. When Hughes writes about segregation or lynching, you can still experience his writing through your own view of the topic, but you must remember to attempt to understand and approach the topic in the context of his time and place.

In the course of planning and drafting your essay, you will want to move past simply summarizing what you have read about the history and context and move toward building an argument of your own. Arguments do not simply spring fully developed from your mind but must be methodically constructed. The more that you read, the more that you may find to assist you in supporting your thesis. Historical and contextualizing information—when it is well chosen and relevant—makes an argument more compelling. Of course, you will want to remember that history and context should usually remain secondary to your analysis of the primary material, the work or works by Hughes that make up the main focus of your essay.

Sample Topics:

1. **The Harlem Renaissance:** Explore how Hughes and his early works fit within the context of the Harlem Renaissance, the artistic movement or period of the 1920s and early 1930s. Narrow your topic to address a specific issue that can be fully discussed in your essay.

   You may want to begin with some background reading on the Harlem Renaissance. Make the effort to locate one or two reputable studies rather than relying simply on the brief, often underdeveloped and unsupported summaries that can be found on the Internet. David Levering Lewis's *When Harlem Was in Vogue* remains one of the standard reference books on this topic. A second volume by Lewis, *The Portable Harlem Renaissance Reader*, offers a solid introductory essay to this period or movement as well as a wide selection of primary materials written by leading figures of the Harlem Renaissance. Narrow your topic to something specific and manageable.

   For example, in reading about the Harlem Renaissance, you might note how much attention Hughes received as a young poet and how many of the hopes of the Harlem Renaissance were placed on his shoulders. You might then begin to ask if one or more particular works by Hughes embody the spirit of the "New Negro," as defined by Alain Locke in his foundational essay, "Enter the New Negro." You may even want to argue that Locke and others came to treat Hughes as a sort of longed-for messiah figure. You may add even more argument to your essay, for example, by demonstrating that the intense focus on Hughes by many of his contemporaries and by many of the critics writing about the Harlem Renaissance decades later has resulted in a distorted view of what the Harlem Renaissance really was about. Perhaps you will find other Harlem Renaissance writers who produced work that you find equal to Hughes's but who rarely receive the same attention as him. You may follow the direction of the feminist scholar Gloria T. Hull, for example, who argues that female authors were rarely given the same support and recognition as Hughes and many of their male contemporaries. This particular contention about neglected women writers gains convincing power because the critic builds her argument by quoting and analyzing some of the correspondence between Locke and other male writers of the Harlem Renaissance.

2. **Literary modernism:** Explore how Hughes and his works fit (or do not fit) within Anglo-American literary modernism, a transatlantic artistic movement or period of the 1920s and 1930s that includes widely read authors such as T.S. Eliot, Virginia Woolf, and Ernest Hemingway.

You may want to begin with some background reading on literary modernism. Again, make the effort to locate one or two reputable studies rather than rely simply on the brief, often underdeveloped and unsupported summaries that can be found everywhere on the Internet. Peter Gay's *Modernism: The Lure of Heresy* offers one recent treatment of the topic and centers on two key components: the modernist artist radically breaks with artistic conventions and engages in intense introspection. You may also want to review Houston A. Baker's studies *Modernism and the Harlem Renaissance* and *Afro-American Poetics: Revisions of Harlem and the Black Aesthetic.*

You may analyze Hughes's writings to see if they contain many of the characteristics of literary modernism, including stylistic innovation, collapsing of high and low cultures, and overt treatment of sexuality and other previously forbidden topics.

3. **The Red Scare and McCarthyism:** Explore the reasons why Hughes was called to testify in front of the House Un-American Activities Committee or why he was scrutinized by the Federal Bureau of Investigation. You may also wish to include a discussion of the effect of those experiences on his future career.

Read or reread several of Hughes's writings from the 1930s, such as the poems "Goodbye Christ" and "One More 'S' in the U.S.A." as well as the essay "To Negro Writers," paying particular attention to what these works have to say about the need for social change in the United States and in the world as well as what they suggest about the role that art might play in bringing about that change. Most of the studies of McCarthyism or the Red Scare that discuss art focus on Hollywood film, but literature was also the subject of intense scrutiny. Read about McCarthyism and the Red Scare in general or perhaps focus more specifically on the FBI's particular scrutiny of black intellectuals in the first half of the 20th century. To get a general understanding of the Red Scare and McCarthyism, you might begin by reviewing the introduction and some of the brief, original documents presented in A. Fried's *McCarthyism: The Great American Red Scare: A Documentary History.* To understand that period in American history and culture in terms of how it affected black people in particular and their struggle for equal rights, look for Jeff Wood's *Black Struggle, Red Scare: Segregation and Anti-Communism in the South, 1948–1968.*

Philosophy and Ideas

Writing on Hughes presents a number of opportunities for exploring philosophy and ideas in one or more than one of his texts. The two sample topics given below both address an abstract question that might be formulated as follows: "Which Hughes are we talking about here?" This question comes from a point of view that holds that we can never fully and wholly understand something as it truly is, that a person like Hughes, for example, will always be understood or presented differently for different reasons and to different audiences. Background reading may help you develop this approach to his writing, but whether this particular point of view was arrived at through one theoretical model or another—perhaps through structuralist or Marxist literary theory or through the notion in psychology of schema—may not be all that important to your essay in the final analysis. What is important is that you think about the question being posed (and make that question clear to the reader) as much as you think about the ways in which you might go about answering that question as fully as possible. There are many other possible philosophies or ideas to explore through Hughes's writings, including Marxism, Afrocentrism, and negritude.

Sample Topics:

1. **Hughes's sexuality:** Biographers and critics have disagreed and continue to disagree over the question of whether or not Hughes was gay. Review some of the different positions, analyze their arguments, and explore what you think we can learn from these ongoing disagreements.

Gay men frequently claim Hughes as one of their own; for examples, see the works listed at the end of this chapter by Devon W. Carbado, Isaac Julien, and Alden Reimonenq. On the other side of the argument, although certainly not alone, is the biographer Arnold Rampersad. Each side frequently reacts in hostile fashion to the other. Rampersad suggests that attempting to read Hughes as gay distorts the truth about the poet. He writes in one part of the biography that a particular poem by Hughes, titled "F.S.," is "sometimes taken insensitively as proof of his homosexual feeling" (62). Rampersad rejects others' quick inferences about Hughes's sexuality in passing, even as he combs through the biographical details to construct his own uncertain accounts of Hughes's sexuality, which he sees at one point as suggestive of a "psycho-sexual complication of a kind far more rare than homosexuality" (46), an assertion he questions more than once, remaining uncertain as to "whether or not Hughes was a homosexual" (66) and "whether [or not] his appetite was normal and adult" (69). Alden Reimonenq counters with less equivocation: "For Rampersad and others who refuse to read between the lines in order to elucidate the facts of Hughes' life, it is clear that a political agenda is operative" ("Hughes, Langston"). John Edgar Tidwell reviews the debate in his essay "The Sounds of Silence," as does A.B. Christa Schwarz in chapter 4 of her book-length study *Gay Voices of the Harlem Renaissance.*

After examining the arguments and evidence presented on both sides, for example, you may find that neither those arguing for or against Hughes being gay has managed to prove their case, that both sides are merely inferring, in one way or another, and remain willfully entrenched in their own position even as they accuse the other camp of deliberately ignoring the evidence, simplifying Hughes's works, or distorting the truth about his life. Having worked through the debate, you may now find yourself in a position to comment more generally on related topics, such as the high level of personal investment that a reader can have in a particular author or the difficulty—if not impossibility—of reading without a "political agenda" of one's own.

2. **Hughes for children or Hughes for adults:** Hughes is an immensely popular subject for books written specifically for children or adolescents. Review one or more of these books for younger audiences. Analyze the content of the book or books and explore what you can learn from the packaging and presentation of Hughes for younger and older audiences.

See the listing of books that are presented at the end of this chapter in the section "Children's Literature and Hughes," including three adult studies of Hughes's writing for children and adolescents by Giselle Liza Anatol, Rudine Sims Bishop, and Katharine Capshaw Smith. By comparing several books on Hughes that are written primarily for children, you may be able to identify significant patterns. You may choose to develop your argument more fully by contrasting what you have found in these books for younger audiences with the content of one or more challenging studies written for adult readers. For example, you may wish to explore why certain moments or achievements in Hughes's life are discussed in detail in books for one audience but not in books for another. You may also find yourself in a good position to comment more generally on what it means to be a child reader or an adult reader.

3. **Marxism, Afrocentrism, or negritude:** Hughes's writings are connected with a number of influential philosophies of the 20th century, including Marxism, Afrocentrism, and negritude. Analyze one or more of Hughes's works in light of one of these philosophies, literary movements, or ideological systems of thought.

   Choose one of these philosophies and conduct research on some of that philosophy's history and core set of principles. Apply what you have learned to one or more of Hughes's works, taking care whenever possible to keep your discussion in your essay grounded in the concrete example or examples of Hughes's writings. For a fuller discussion of these topics, see the suggestions presented at the end of the chapters on the poems "The Negro Speaks of Rivers" and "Goodbye Christ."

Form and Genre

Form and genre involve the structure of a literary work and the literary tradition, if any, that the work draws on or references. In the case of Hughes, one common genre is lyric poetry, and one common form is free verse. Lyric poetry is generally defined as poetry that does not have as its main concern the telling of a story (it is not epic, dramatic, or narrative poetry) but rather seeks to express the speaker's emotions. Free verse is poetry that does not follow a strict meter or rhyme scheme and that often contains lines that vary greatly in length. In his free verse, Hughes uses techniques other than regular meter, rhyme, and line length to achieve coherence, including the repetition of key words and phrases. Form and genre are an integral part of any literary text. Works of literature do not appear out of nowhere, and every work can be understood in relation to one or more literary traditions—whether the work seeks to fit within the tradition, seeks to modify the tradition, or seeks to reject the tradition outright.

Sample Topics:

1. **Lyric poetry or protest poetry:** Characterize the forms or genres that might best characterize Hughes's poetry. Lyric poetry may be defined as poems that focus on the refined emotions or perceptions of a solitary speaker. Protest poetry may be defined as poems that are inherently less refined in their content, that are written in response to an injustice, and that frequently seek to mobilize the reader to action. You may wish to read other definitions of these two types of poetry or develop definitions of your own.

   In the introduction to the third volume of *The Collected Works of Langston Hughes,* Arnold Rampersad's summary of Hughes's poetic career suggests that lyric poetry and protest poetry are two separate genres of poetry or, at the very least, two extremes on a poetic spectrum:

   > As a poet, Hughes had demonstrated time and again a flexibility of temperament and technique that allowed him to establish a solid reputation as a lyric poet of unusual charm and, at the same time, as a highly effective social and political poet. His range stretched from earnest depictions of aspects of nature and loneliness to the most radical expressions of outrage against the inhumanities of racism and unbridled capitalism. (1)

   Review a selection of Hughes's poetry, not just the poems presented in one volume (such as just those in the 1959 *Selected Poems* edition, a volume that contains little of Hughes's more radical poems), and write about the range of Hughes's poetry. You may wish to use this topic as an opportunity to engage James Baldwin's assessment in his review of the 1959 volume *Selected Poems of Langston Hughes* that "Hughes is at his best" when writing short, lyric poems such as "The Negro Speaks of Rivers" and "Dream Variations" (qtd. in Bloom, *Langston Hughes,* 41).

2. **Autobiographies and biographical parallels:** Identify and explore meaningful connections between Hughes's literary works and his life.

Although Hughes's works may not appear to be very autobiographical at first, many of them can be seen as veiled retellings of and commentaries on the author's personal experiences and struggles. Read about Hughes's childhood, family life, writing career, and related topics in the biographies by Faith Berry and Arnold Rampersad. Because biographies are often extensive, you may wish to use the tables of contents and indexes to find the sections relevant to your area of interest. You may then compare some of what you have learned about Hughes's life to one or more themes or characters in his poetry or fiction or to the arguments in one or more of his essays. Determine if there is a connection that resonates powerfully for you. If so, explore this connection to determine how it may help you better understand both the literary work and the author. Several critics have observed that some of Hughes's poetry (such as "The Negro Speaks of Rivers") and fiction (such as "Father and Son") may be seen as reflections or reimaginings of his antagonistic relationship with his father. Similarly, the poem "Mother to Son" and the short story "Thank You, Ma'am" might be read as literary revisions of his conflicted relationship with his mother.

3. **Art or folklore:** Explore the claims by Countee Cullen and Leroi Jones, among others, that Hughes may be less an inventive artist than a collector of folklore.

Cullen's comments come from his review of Hughes's first volume of poetry, *The Weary Blues,* while Jones's observations are contained in his review of Hughes's second novel, *Tambourines to Glory.* You will want to read Cullen's or Jones's full review carefully and identify their main assertions about the shortcomings of Hughes as a writer in general and of the work under discussion in particular. After working through the short reviews and checking the critics' assertions against your own understanding of the author and his works, you will be in a good position to write a paper that agrees or disagrees with some or all of Cullen's or Jones's main points and central arguments.

Language, Symbols, and Imagery

Hughes's poetry may appear deceptively simple and perhaps even undeserving of a close reading. Your careful attention to his use of language, symbols, and imagery may counter this initial reaction and may lead you to new insights about the writer and his works. Chapter one presents a brief overview of some key terms and concepts related to imagery, figurative language, and symbolism.

Sample Topics:

1. **The mountain, the moon, or the dream deferred:** Identify a significant image or phrase that appears more than once in Hughes's writings. Analyze the importance of that image or phrase to each individual work in which it appears and then go on to discuss how the meaning of that image or phrase remains constant or changes in meaning from work to work.

Possible recurring items to focus on include the image of the mountain, the image of the moon, or the term *dream deferred.* In writing about the image of the mountain, you may consider focusing on the essay "The Negro Artist and the Racial Mountain" and the poem "Crossing," in which the speaker talks about going "up on the mountain" with other people and yet continues to feel alone. In writing about the image of the moon, you may consider reading Hughes's essay "To Negro Writers" as well as a range of his early and later works in order to explore how in his essay from the early 1930s Hughes dismisses poems about the moon as irrelevant and yet includes in both his first volume of poetry as well as in his later volume *Fields of Wonder* (1947) a number of poems in which the moon figures prominently. In writing about the phrase *dream deferred*, you may consider focusing on the poems in Hughes's 1951 volume *Montage of a Dream Deferred* and exploring both how the phrase is incorporated into individual poems and, in the course of reading the poems, how the phrase becomes a unifying motif for the volume as a whole. Additional topics include the colors black and white (and all the colors in between), the cabaret, suicide, the dream, and the song.

2. **Recycled language and irony:** A number of Hughes's poems cleverly reuse language from a source—usually but not always a source from the dominant white culture—in order to offer ironic commentary.

Hughes draws language not just from popular African-American culture but also from the dominant culture, which would seek to exclude him from full membership. Attention to the language in Hughes's poems, for example, will allow you to hear and appreciate his subtle incorporation of lyrics from the traditional Confederate song "Dixie" in "Song for a Dark Girl," his much less subtle use of marketing language in "Advertisement for the Waldorf-Astoria," or his use of the ending of the Pledge of Allegiance in "Children's Rhymes." Look for similarly ironic or an otherwise critical reuse of language in his other poems. In an essay on this topic, you may want to identify and review the source or sources that Hughes borrows from while critiquing it at the same time. After analyzing the individual poems, you can work toward a general statement of your own about Hughes's use of recycled language and irony. You may be interested, for example, in demonstrating that Hughes was not the first African-American poet to use this strategy; you may want to explore how James M. Whitfield's 1853 poem "America" similarly appropriates many words and phrases (and perhaps even an alternative title) from the 1831 lyrics to the patriotic hymn "My Country, 'Tis of Thee" in order to sharply criticize the United States for failing to live up to its own ideals of liberty and equality for all. To cite more parodies of that particular song and other patriotic hymns by abolitionists, see chapter three of Timothy E. Scheurer's *Born in the U.S.A.: The Myth of America in Popular Music from Colonial Times to the Present.* To explore this artistic strategy more fully, you may wish to read dictionary or reference book entries on (or even longer theoretical discussions of) the technique of parody. Consult, for example, the summary of Linda Hutcheon's extensive discussions of parody, which is available online at the Introductory Guide to Critical Theory.

Compare and Contrast Essays

When writing a compare and contrast essay, you will want to remember that your essay should do a great deal more than merely point out similarities and differences among two or more things related to Hughes. It is your job to explain to your readers the significance of these similarities and differences, to turn your observations into a strong, coherent interpretation or argument. This task will be easier if you have a good reason for comparing the pieces that you are discussing in the first place. For example, if you compare and contrast the poem "The Weary Blues" with the short story "The Blues I'm Playing" because they are both by Hughes and because both works deal with black blues musicians, then your observations of the similarities and differences between these two works will likely enable you to draw meaningful conclusions about Hughes's views of this particular type of artist or perhaps even his views of the black artist in general. Likewise, if you compare and contrast Hughes's essays "The Negro Artist and the Racial Mountain" and "To Negro Writers"— because they both discuss the pressures on and responsibilities of the black artist in the first half of the 20th century but come to different conclusions about the proper subject of poetry—then you will likely be able to develop a compelling argument in regard to Hughes's changing ideas of what it means to be an artist who creates with integrity.

Sample Topics:

1. **A different Hughes for different audiences:** Explore how Hughes, more than most writers, may have tailored his work to fit different audiences.

   In her biography, Faith Berry observes: "Throughout much of his career, Hughes wrote differently for different audiences—one for his commercial books, another for noncommercial magazines. The duality at times made him look like a chameleon, a cop-out" (286). Explore this idea of finding a different Hughes whenever he is specifically writing for a different audience. You may want to focus initially on the differences between two volumes of poetry separated by only one year, *Shakespeare in Harlem* (1942) and *Jim Crow's Last Stand* (1943). The first of these two volumes was published by Knopf, Hughes's mainstream publishing house, and the second appeared as a pamphlet published by the much less mainstream, leftist Negro Publication Society of America. After reviewing some or all of the poems in the two volumes, you may wish to compare and contrast specific poems from each. Arnold Rampersad writes that, in the first volume, Hughes "sidestepped politics in favor of blues and humor" and that the second volume "captured a much angrier and more politically engaged poet" (Hughes, *The Collected Works of Langston Hughes* 2: 4, 5). These statements by two important scholars on Hughes—Berry and Rampersad—may provide you with additional points to discuss in your essay. Do you agree with Rampersad that the blues and humor poems in the first volume indeed avoid political issues? Do you agree with Berry that Hughes may indeed have appeared to be (or, in fact, have been) "a chameleon, a cop-out" because he tailored his work to fit his different audiences?

2. **Other continuities (or discontinuities) in Hughes's works:** In a manner similar to the first suggested topic in this section, compare and contrast another aspect of Hughes's writing, such as a certain style of writing or a certain theme, in two or more of his works. The following discussion of this sample topic focuses on Hughes's use of popular black musical forms in his poetry throughout his career.

You will want to start by choosing two or more texts by Hughes that seem to you to have interesting and significant connections. For example, you may observe that the poems contained in the volumes *Fine Clothes to the Jew* (1927) and *Montage of a Dream Deferred* (1951) take both their form and content from black popular music, but the blues lyrics that Hughes gives so much attention to in the first volume are replaced by later musical forms—particularly boogie-woogie and bebop—in the later volume. You might compare and contrast selected poems from these two volumes, focusing on how Hughes makes use of black popular music. How, exactly, does Hughes incorporate music into poems in the two volumes? Is there a difference in how he does this, or does his technique remain pretty much the same? Does it matter that the type of music has changed? In this approach, you may begin by analyzing the centrality of black popular music in each individual poem that you have selected and then set your analyses of the poems side by side and draw more general conclusions about the use of black popular music in the poems in both volumes. Based on your analyses, you may go on to generalize about Hughes's position toward popular black music. Alternatively, you may want to compare and contrast several poems or short stories that feature black writers or other artists, noting whether this type of character changes over the course of the poems or short stories or remains relatively static. For example, you may explore how the musician who appears in the poem "The Weary Blues" is similar to or different from the musician who appears in the short story "The Blues I'm Playing."

3. **Works by Hughes and another artist:** Compare and contrast Hughes's work with that of another artist.

Begin by choosing another artist and work or set of works based on meaningful similarities and differences. The other artist, for example, may be a second famous black poet of the Harlem Renaissance, such as Countee Cullen or Claude McKay. Alternately, the other artist may have lived in a different time but still share strong commonalities with Hughes, such as Walt Whitman or Paul Laurence Dunbar. A final option would be to consider an artist who had strong and famous conflicts with Hughes, such as Zora Neale Hurston or Leroi Jones (also known as Amiri Baraka).

You may decide to compare and contrast Countee Cullen's "Yet Do I Marvel" and Hughes's "The Weary Blues," for example, because they both address the theme of black creativity in the 1920s. Or you may decide to compare and contrast Walt Whitman's "I Hear America Singing" and Hughes's "I, Too, Sing America"; the two poets lived in different periods and have different backgrounds, but their poetry often employs similar structures and themes. Or you may decide to compare and contrast poems by Hughes with those by Jones; in the mid-1960s, Hughes's poetic career was nearing its end just as

Jones's was on the rise, and the two poets disagreed strongly over the form and function of modern black poetry.

In general, if you come to see the artists and their works as having more interesting and meaningful similarities than differences, you may want to focus on analyzing those commonalities. You might explore, for example, how Hughes's poetry seems an extension of Whitman's project in *Leaves of Grass*. On the other hand, if the differences seem more interesting and meaningful to you than the similarities, then you may want to shift your focus to describing the differences and drawing out their implications. You might explore how Hughes and Cullen, both important figures in the Harlem Renaissance, differ in their views of what it means to be black and a poet in the 1920s and early 1930s.

Bibliography and Online Resources

Anderson, Jervis. *This Was Harlem: A Cultural Portrait, 1900–1950.* New York: Farrar, Straus and Giroux, 1981.

Avi-Ram, Amitai F. "The Unreadable Black Body: 'Conventional' Poetic Form in the Harlem Renaissance." *Genders* 7 (1990): 32–45.

Baker, Houston A. *Afro-American Poetics: Revisions of Harlem and the Black Aesthetic.* Madison: U of Wisconsin P, 1988.

———. *Modernism and the Harlem Renaissance.* Chicago: U of Chicago P, 1987.

Barksdale, Richard K. *Langston Hughes: The Poet and His Critics.* Chicago: American Library Association, 1977.

Bell, Bernard W. *The Afro-American Novel and Its Tradition.* Amherst: U of Massachusetts P, 1987.

Bernard, Emily. *Remember Me to Harlem: The Letters of Langston Hughes and Carl Van Vechten, 1925–1964.* New York: Alfred A. Knopf, 2001.

Berry, Faith. *Langston Hughes: Before and Beyond Harlem.* Westport, Conn.: Lawrence Hill, 1983.

Bloom, Harold, ed. *Langston Hughes.* New York: Chelsea House, 1989.

———, ed. *Langston Hughes.* Bloom's Major Poets. Broomall, Penn.: Chelsea House, 1999.

———. *Langston Hughes.* New York: Chelsea House, 2001.

Bonner, Pat E. *Sassy Jazz and Slo' Draggin' Blues: Music in the Poetry of Langston Hughes.* New York: P. Lang, 1996.

Bontemps, Arna. *The Harlem Renaissance Remembered.* New York: Dodd, Mead, 1972.

Carbado, Devon W., Dwight A. McBride, and Donald Weise. *Black Like Us: A Century of Lesbian, Gay, and Bisexual African American Fiction.* San Francisco: Cleis Press, 2002.

Carroll, Anne Elizabeth. *Word, Image, and the New Negro: Representation and Identity in the Harlem Renaissance.* Bloomington: Indiana UP, 2005.

Cobb, Martha. *Harlem, Haiti, and Havana: A Comparative Critical Study of Langston Hughes, Jaques Romain, Nicolas Guillen.* Washington, D.C.: Three Continents P, 1979.

Cullen, Countee. Review of *The Weary Blues. Langston Hughes.* Ed. Harold Bloom. Broomall, Penn.: Chelsea House, 1999. 18–20.

Dace, Tish. *Langston Hughes: The Contemporary Reviews.* New York: Cambridge UP, 1997.

Dickinson, Donald C. *A Bio-Bibliography of Langston Hughes, 1902–1967.* 2nd rev. ed. Hamden, Conn.: Archon Books, 1972.

Duberman, Martin. Ed. *Re/Membering Langston.* New York: New York UP, 1997.

Duffy, Susan, ed. *The Political Plays of Langston Hughes.* Carbondale, Ill.: Southern Illinois UP, 2000.

Emanuel, James A. *Langston Hughes.* Boston: Twayne, 1967.

Fabre, Michel. *From Harlem to Paris: Black American Writers in France, 1840–1980.* Urbana: University of Illinois Press, 1991.

Fried, A. *McCarthyism: The Great American Red Scare: A Documentary History.* New York: Oxford UP, 1997.

Gates, Henry Louis, Jr., and Gene Andrew Jarrett, eds. *The New Negro: Readings on Race, Representation, and African American Culture, 1892–1938.* Princeton, N.J.: Princeton UP, 2007.

Gates, Henry Louis, Jr., and K. A. Appiah. *Langston Hughes: Critical Perspectives Past and Present.* New York: Amistad, 1993.

Gay, Peter. *Modernism: The Lure of Heresy.* New York: W.W. Norton, 2007.

Gibson, Donald B. *Five Black Writers: Essays on Wright, Ellison, Baldwin, Hughes and Le Roi Jones.* New York: New York UP, 1970.

Harper, Donna S. *Not So Simple: The "Simple" Stories by Langston Hughes.* Columbia: U of Missouri P, 1995.

Haskins, James. *Always Movin' On: The Life of Langston Hughes.* Trenton, N.J.: Africa World Press, 1993.

Huggins, Nathan. *Harlem Renaissance.* New York: Oxford UP, 1971.

Hughes, Langston. *The Collected Works of Langston Hughes.* Columbia: U of Missouri P, 2002. 16 vols.

Hutchinson, George. *The Harlem Renaissance in Black and White*. Cambridge: Harvard UP, 1995.

Hull, Gloria T. *Color, Sex, and Poetry: Three Women Writers of the Harlem Renaissance*. Bloomington: Indiana UP, 1987.

Inge, M. Thomas, Maurice Duke, and Jackson R. Bryer. *Black American Writers: Bibliographical Essays, I: The Beginnings through the Harlem Renaissance and Langston Hughes*. New York: St. Martin's, 1978.

Jemie, Onwuchekwa. *Langston Hughes: An Introduction to the Poetry*. New York: Columbia UP, 1976.

Jones, Leroi. "*Tambourines to Glory*." *The Jazz Review* 2 (June 1959): 33–34. "*Tambourines to Glory*, Langston Hughes, 1958." *Novels for Students*. Vol. 21. Ed. Ira Milne and Timothy Sisler. Detroit: Thomson Gale, 2005. 286–89.

Kellner, Bruce, ed. *The Harlem Renaissance: A Historical Dictionary for the Era*. New York: Methuen, 1984.

Kramer, Victor A., ed. *The Harlem Renaissance Re-Examined*. New York: AMS Press, 1987.

Larson, Norita D. *Langston Hughes, Poet of Harlem*. Mankato, Minn.: Creative Education, 1981.

Lewis, David L., ed. and intro. *The Portable Harlem Renaissance Reader*. New York: Penguin, 1995.

———. *When Harlem Was in Vogue*. New York: Penguin, 1997.

Looking for Langston: A Meditation on Langston Hughes and the Harlem Renaissance with the Poetry of Essex Hemphill and Bruce Nugent. Sankofa Film & Video. Written and directed by Isaac Julien. Producer Nadine Marsh-Edwards. New York: Water Bearer Films, 1992.

Lown, Fredric. *Langston Hughes: An Interdisciplinary Biography*. Portland, Maine: J. Weston Walch, 1997.

Mandelik, Peter. *A Concordance to the Poetry of Langston Hughes*. Detroit: Gale Research, 1975.

Maxwell, William J. *New Negro, Old Left: African American Writing and Communism between the Wars*. New York: Columbia UP, 1999.

McLaren, Joseph. *Form and Feeling: The Critical Reception of Edward Kennedy, Duke Ellington, and Langston Hughes 1920–1966*. New York: Taylor & Francis, 1995.

———. *Langston Hughes: Folk Dramatist in the Protest Tradition, 1921–1943*. Westport, Conn.: Greenwood P, 1997.

Mikolyzk, Thomas A. *Langston Hughes: A Bio-Bibliography*. New York: Greenwood P, 1990.

Miller, R. Baxter. *The Art and Imagination of Langston Hughes.* Lexington: UP of Kentucky, 1989.

——. *Langston Hughes and Gwendolyn Brooks: A Reference Guide.* Boston: G. K. Hall, 1978.

Mullen, Edward J. *Critical Essays on Langston Hughes.* Boston: G. K. Hall, 1986.

——, ed. *Langston Hughes in the Hispanic World and Haiti.* Hamden, Conn.: Archon, 1977.

O'Daniel, Therman B., ed. *Langston Hughes: Black Genius—A Critical Evaluation.* New York: Morrow, 1971.

Ostrom, Hans. *Langston Hughes: A Study of the Short Fiction.* New York: Twayne, 1993.

——. *A Langston Hughes Encyclopedia.* Westport: Greenwood, 2002.

Rampersad, Arnold. *The Life of Langston Hughes.* Vol. 1. *1902–1941: I, Too, Sing America.* New York: Oxford UP, 2002.

——. *The Life of Langston Hughes.* Vol. 2. *1941–1967: I Dream a World.* New York: Oxford UP, 2002.

——. "The Origins of Poetry in Langston Hughes." *The Southern Review* 21:3 (1985): 694–705.

Redding, Saunders J. *To Make a Poet Black.* Chapel Hill: U of North Carolina P, 1939.

Ross, Marlon Bryan. *Manning the Race: Reforming Black Men in the Jim Crow Era.* New York: New York UP, 2004.

Rummel, Jack. *Langston Hughes.* Intro. Coretta Scott King. New York: Chelsea House, 1988.

Scheurer, Timothy E. *Born in the U.S.A.: The Myth of America in Popular Music from Colonial Times to the Present.* Jackson: UP of Mississippi, 2007.

Schwarz, A.B. Christa. *Gay Voices of the Harlem Renaissance.* Bloomington: Indiana UP, 2003.

Singh, Amritjit, S. William Shiver, and Stanley Brodwin, eds. *The Harlem Renaissance: Revaluations.* New York: Garland, 1989.

Smethurst, James Edward. *The Black Arts Movement: Literary Nationalism in the 1960s and 1970s.* Chapel Hill: U of North Carolina P, 2005.

——. *The New Red Negro: The Literary Left and African American Poetry, 1930–1946.* New York: Oxford UP, 1999.

Story, Ralph D. "Patronage and the Harlem Renaissance: You Get What You Pay For." *College Language Association Journal* 32.3 (1989). 284–95.

Thurman, Wallace. *Infants of the Spring.* New York: Macaulay, 1932.

Tidwell, John Edgar, Arnold Rampersad, and Cheryl R. Ragar, ed. and intro. *Montage of a Dream: The Art and Life of Langston Hughes.* Columbia: U of Missouri P, 2007.

Tidwell, John Edgar. "The Sounds of Silence: Langston Hughes as a 'Down Low' Brother?" *Montage of a Dream: The Art and Life of Langston Hughes.* Ed. John Edgar Tidwell, Cheryl R. Ragar, and Arnold Rampersad. Columbia: U of Missouri P, 2007. 55–67.

Tracy, Steven C. *A Historical Guide to Langston Hughes.* New York: Oxford UP, 2004.

———. *Langston Hughes and the Blues.* Urbana: U of Illinois P, 1988.

Trotman, C. James, ed. *Langston Hughes: The Man, His Art and His Continuing Influence.* New York: Garland, 1995.

Wagner, Jean. *Black Poets of the United States: From Paul Laurence Dunbar to Langston Hughes.* Trans. Kenneth Douglass. Urbana: U of Illinois P, 1973.

Wintz, Cary D. *Black Culture and the Harlem Renaissance.* Houston: Rice University Press, 1983.

Wintz, Cary D., and Paul Finkelman, eds. *Encyclopedia of the Harlem Renaissance.* New York: Routledge, 2004. 2 vols.

Wood, Jeff. *Black Struggle, Red Scare: Segregation and Anti-Communism in the South, 1948–1968.* Baton Rouge: Louisiana State UP, 2004.

Online Resources

Felluga, Dino. "Introduction to Linda Hutcheon: Module on Parody." Introductory Guide to Critical Theory. http://www.cla.purdue.edu/English/theory/postmodernism/modules/hutcheonparody.html. 28 November 2003. Downloaded on February 26, 2009.

Harlem: 1900–1940 Schomburg Center for Research in Black Culture, The New York Public Library. http://www.si.umich.edu/chico/Harlem/. April 2001. Downloaded on February 26, 2009.

"Harlem: Mecca of the New Negro." *Survey Graphic.* March 1925. http://etext.virginia.edu/harlem/. 3 November 1996. Downloaded on February 26, 2009.

Kresh, David. "Langston Hughes and His Poetry." September 12, 2003. The Library of Congress Webcasts. Available online at The Library of Congress. URL: www.loc.gov/today/cyberlc/feature_wdesc.php?rec-3352. Downloaded on March 3, 2009.

"Langston Hughes." Academy of American Poets. Available online at www.poets.org. URL: http://www.poets.org/poet.php/prmPID/83. 2009. Downloaded on March 3, 2009.

"Modern American Poetry: Langston Hughes." Modern American Poetry: An Online Journal and Multimedia Companion to *Anthology of Modern American Poetry*. Ed. Cary Nelson. http://www.english.illinois.edu/maps/poets/g_l/hughes/hughes.htm. Downloaded on March 3, 2009.

Reimonenq, Alden. "Hughes, Langston." *glbtq: An Encyclopedia of Gay, Lesbian, Bisexual, Transgender, and Queer Culture*. Ed. Claude J. Summers. www.glbtq.com/literature/hughes_l.html. 2002. Downloaded on February 22, 2009.

Children's Literature and Hughes

Anatol, Giselle Liza. "Langston Hughes and the Children's Literary Tradition." *Montage of a Dream: The Art and Life of Langston Hughes*. Ed. John Edgar Tidwell, Arnold Rampersad, and Cheryl R. Ragar. Columbia: U of Missouri P, 2007. 237–58.

Bishop, Rudine Sims. *Free within Ourselves: The Development of African American Children's Literature*. Santa Barbara, Calif.: Greenwood P, 2007.

Burleigh, Robert. *Langston's Train Ride*. New York: Orchard Books, 2004.

Cooper, Floyd. *Coming Home: From the Life of Langston Hughes*. New York: Philomel Books, 1994.

Dunham, Montrew. *Langston Hughes: Young Black Poet*. New York: Aladdin Paperbacks, 1995.

Hill, Christine. *Langston Hughes: Poet of the Harlem Renaissance*. Springfield, N.J.: Enslow, 1997.

McKissack, Pat, *Langston Hughes: Great American Poet*. Springfield, N.J.: Enslow, 2002

Medina, Tony. *Love to Langston*. New York: Lee & Low Books, 2002.

Myers, Elisabeth P. *Langston Hughes: Poet of his People*. Champaign, Ill.: Garrard P, 1970.

Perdomo, Willie. *Visiting Langston*. New York: Henry Holt and Co., 2002.

Raatma, Lucia. *Langston Hughes*. Minneapolis: Child's World, 2002.

Roessel, David, and Arnold Rampersad, eds. *Langston Hughes*. New York: Sterling P, 2006.

Smith, Katharine Capshaw. *Children's Literature of the Harlem Renaissance*. Bloomington: Indiana UP, 2004.

Walker, Alice. *Langston Hughes: American Poet*. New York: Amistad, 2002.

Wallace, Maurice O. *Langston Hughes: The Harlem Renaissance*. Tarrytown, N.Y.: Marshall Cavendish Benchmark, 2008.

"THE NEGRO SPEAKS OF RIVERS"

READING TO WRITE

THE PUBLICATION of "The Negro Speaks of Rivers" in June 1921 in *The Crisis*, the journal of the NAACP edited by W.E.B. Du Bois, marks the beginning of Langston Hughes's long and productive writing career. The poem reappeared in print several times in years that followed, including in *The Literary Digest* (July 2, 1921) and in Hughes's first book-length collection of poetry, *The Weary Blues* (1926), where it carried a dedication to Du Bois. As Arnold Rampersad writes in the introduction to volume one of *The Collected Works of Langston Hughes*, the poet viewed "The Negro Speaks of Rivers" as his "signature poem" and often saved it for the final poem when reading his work for the public (Hughes, *The Collected Works of Langston Hughes* 1:3). Today, this early poem remains perhaps the most widely taught and most widely anthologized work by Hughes.

In *The Big Sea*, the first volume of his autobiography, Hughes gives a detailed account of the spontaneous process of composing this poem while traveling to join his father in Mexico:

Now it was just sunset, and we crossed the Mississippi, slowly, over a long bridge. I looked out the window of the Pullman at the great muddy river flowing down toward the heart of the South, and I began to think what that river, the old Mississippi, had meant to Negroes in the past—how to be sold down the river was the worst fate that could overtake a slave in times of bondage. Then I remembered reading how Abraham Lincoln had made a trip down the Mississippi on a raft to New Orleans, and how he had seen slavery at its worst, and had decided within himself that it should be removed from American life. Then I began to think about other rivers in our past—the Congo, and the Niger, and the Nile in Africa—and the thought came to me: "I've known rivers," and I put it down on the back of an envelope I had in my pocket, and within the space of ten or fifteen minutes, as the train gathered speed in the dusk, I had written this poem, which I called "The Negro Speaks of Rivers." (65–66)

Hughes was a young man when he wrote this poem. He had not yet been to Africa, and what he presents in "The Negro Speaks of Rivers" is not so much a record of his engagement with the actual continent than it is his meditation on a romanticized, mythic land that has its origins in his own imagination. Despite these limitations, however, Hughes's poem has enduring value. Critics often praise this early poem for, to use Lorenzo Thomas's words, "creat[ing] the universal and eternal Negro whose modern situation differs from antiquity primarily in the loss of power and self-determination" (187).

A rich and resonant work such as "The Negro Speaks of Rivers" can suggest any number of critical approaches. Begin with a close, active reading of the poem—a process that requires close attention and more than one reading of the poem. Read for comprehension first. In your second and later readings, record your comments and reactions. Read the poem aloud at least once to get a better sense of the sounds and patterns in the poem. Because this poem is short, only ten lines in all, you may want to print out a copy or use a reproduction for underlining or highlighting important phrases, repeated words, and related images on your photocopy. Ask questions and make observations about theme and language, perhaps beginning with the first word in the first line: Who is the "I" who opens the poem? Is it simply a black person, as the title of the poem suggests? This person, the speaker in the poem, is featured again at the beginning of eight of the remaining nine lines of the poem, as well as in the poem's title, so clearly this individual is important. What information about this speaker can you gather from the poem? For example: When did this speaker live? What different things has this speaker done? Is this a man or a woman? Is this Langston Hughes? Is this speaker even human?

After asking and answering your questions, as fully as possible, you may refer back to the poem's title and consider whether the poem's title allows for more than one meaning. The speaker may be simply a black person, as you might have first thought, or the speaker may be both that and something more. You may even reflect on the use of the definite article—"*the* negro speaks . . ."—rather than the indefinite article—"*a* negro speaks . . ."—in the poem's title.

You can continue your exploration of the poem by looking for repeated phrases, such as the two appearances of the word *human* in the second line: ". . . older than the flow of human blood in human veins." Additionally, you may look up the different rivers' names in an encyclopedia or geographical dictionary and see what connections you can make between them. Finally, you may consider the meanings and associations of the words that are used to describe the transformation of the Mississippi River in the latter half of line seven, the longest line in the poem: ". . . I've seen its muddy bosom turn all golden in the sunset." At this point, your ideas are most likely broad and undefined, but you will have generated your own reactions and assessments that can be used, in whole or in part, in a focused and developed essay on this poem.

As is the case with many of Hughes's poems, "The Negro Speaks of Rivers" is a short work and uses a simple structure and vocabulary. Thus, even after carefully discussing a number of related elements in the poem, you may find it difficult to write an essay of more than a few pages in length, unless you bring in additional, relevant material. Close reading is a good place to begin when working with Hughes's poetry, but often it is not the place where you will want to end. Review the different topics and strategies in the following section for ideas on how you might develop your paper idea more fully.

TOPICS AND STRATEGIES
Themes

Sample Topics:

1. **Present and past time:** Consider what might make the river a particularly meaningful symbol in "The Negro Speaks of Rivers," a poem that deals with the passage of time and the connections between the present and the past.

   Research at least briefly the four rivers named in the poem "The Negro Speaks of Rivers." Reflect on what these rivers may have in common and why they may be presented in this

particular order in the poem. Consider the possible meanings of the different adjectives used in the poem to modify the
river symbol, including "dusky," "muddy," and "golden." You
may want to consider and respond to the conflicting views of
critics on this topic of the significance of the rivers named in
Hughes's poem. For example, Joyce A. Joyce sees the poem as
"trac[ing] the movement of black life from the Euphrates and
Nile rivers in Africa to the Mississippi" and writes that the
poet "identifies himself and his blackness with the first human
beings" (109). By contrast, George Hutchinson writes that the
poem presents "a pre-racial dawn and a geography far from
Africa that is identified with neither blackness nor whiteness"
(98). Joyce and Hutchinson do not agree on the central theme
of this poem, and you have the opportunity to weigh in with
your own informed position on what this poem is about.

2. **Literal and figurative parents:** Explore the possible indirect
   sources for the poem "The Negro Speaks of Rivers" in Hughes's
   early years. This approach may require particular attention be
   paid to the line in the poem that features both Abraham Lincoln and the Mississippi River's "muddy bosom."

A number of critics, including Jean Wagner and Rachel Blau
DuPlessis, have commented on the literal and figurative mothers and fathers in Hughes's poetry. Wagner focuses on mothers when she writes about the poem, "If he celebrates Africa as
his mother, it is not only because all the black peoples originated there but also because America, which should be his
real mother, had always behaved toward him in stepmotherly
fashion" (395). DuPlessis focuses on fathers when she asserts
that the poem "was written as an internal dialogue with his
father whose 'strange dislike of his own people' baffled and
disturbed Hughes, and, of course, implicated his son as object
of that dislike" (95). If you see Hughes as speaking of himself
in this poem, as both Wagner and DuPlessis do, consider what
treatment he received and what literal and figurative parents
he had as a young black man in the United States in the first
seventeen or eighteen years of his life. On the other hand, if

you see Hughes as speaking for all black Americans, consider what the general status of black Americans was from around 1900 to 1920, the period roughly corresponding to Hughes's formative years up to the time this poem was written and published. Either way, you can use the idea of literal and figurative mothers and/or fathers to structure your essay.

Either approach requires research. For discussion of Hughes's early life and possible connections to his poems, refer to Rampersad's and Berry's biographies. For a more general discussion of the status of black Americans in the first two decades of the 20th century, locate a scholarly and researched book on black cultural history or cultural studies in the modern United States, such as Barbara McCaskill's *Post-bellum, Pre-Harlem: African American Literature and Culture, 1877–1919* or Marlon Bryan Ross's *Manning the Race: Reforming Black Men in the Jim Crow Era.*

3. **Different views of Africa:** Compare and contrast Hughes's treatment of Africa in the poem "The Negro Speaks of Rivers" or other works written early in his career (up to 1930) to his treatment of Africa in works written much later in his career (from the 1950s onward).

Onwuchekwa Jemie has maintained that a new poetics of Africa emerges in Hughes's later work: Africa seems "so much closer, . . . so much more real in *Ask Your Mama* and *The Panther and the Lash*, than, for instance, in *The Weary Blues* or *One-Way Ticket*" (125). Examine a few poems or other works from Hughes's early and late career to determine if you agree with Jemie. Explain in your analysis where the reader can or cannot see this difference in Hughes's increasing closeness to Africa.

Philosophy and Ideas

Sample Topics:

1. **Philosophies of composition:** Explore the story behind Hughes's writing of the poem "The Negro Speaks of Rivers" and consider the usefulness of that story to improving your understanding of the poem.

In addition to the account of the composition of the poem presented in *The Big Sea* and reproduced in the opening section of this chapter, Hughes has given at least three similar but not wholly identical accounts of the composition and meaning of the poem. These recorded accounts—and, no doubt, others—can be found on the Internet and in other media. See the bibliography and list of online resources at the end of this chapter for a listing of the entries for the Poetry Archive, Salon.com, and www.poets.org. You may further develop this essay by including a discussion of how Hughes's accounts resemble or differ from Edgar Allan Poe's famous account of how he wrote "The Raven," as outlined in his widely anthologized essay "Philosophy of Composition." In your essay, you may discuss the similar emphasis on the importance of a recurring line in the poem and the difference in how quickly or slowly the poem developed.

2. **Global reach and negritude:** Use the naming of several of the world's rivers in the poem "The Negro Speaks of Rivers" as an opportunity to explore the global reach of Hughes's poetry. This exploration may lead you to larger questions about Hughes's important role in the development of the intellectual and artistic program known as negritude.

Daniel Won-gu Kim argues that Arnold Rampersad, one of Hughes's main biographers, "overstates Hughes's alienation from Africa" and that

> a careful reading of Rampersad's biography for Hughes' travels to Africa and his relationships with African writers and intellectuals indicates the need for a sustained scholarly examination of Hughes' influence on African literature. The tendency in scholarship has been to focus on the one-way flow of influence, from Africa to America. (437)

Follow Kim's lead by reviewing one or more biographies of Hughes for references to Africa and begin constructing an argument that Hughes influenced Africa (including many of its writers and intellectuals) at least as much as he was influenced by his fantasies of and actual travels to Africa. You may be led to explore and establish connections to Du Bois's idea of pan-Africanism or to review studies on some prominent figures of negritude. See the works listed at the end of this chapter by Edward O. Ako, A. James Arnold, Sylvia Washington Bâ, D. A. Masolo, and Edward J. Mullen. The book by Anita Haya Patterson contains the chapter "From Harlem to Haiti: Langston Hughes, Jacques Roumain and the Avant-Gardes," and the essay listed there by Mbuelelo Vizikhung Vzamane quotes numerous prominent black South African writers stating that they were strongly influenced by several Harlem Renaissance writers, with the names Hughes and Du Bois appearing most frequently. Finally, you may consider Hughes's own promotion of global black identity in the United States and abroad through his poems such as "Always the Same," in his translations of other poets of color, and in his editing of anthologies such as *Poems from Black Africa.*

3. **Black Egypt and Afrocentrism:** Use the references to the Nile and the pyramids in the poem "The Negro Speaks of Rivers" as an opportunity to explore the still unresolved debate over the possibility that Egyptian civilization was predominately a black African culture. This debate may lead you to larger questions and controversies surrounding Afrocentrism.

At first glance, line six of Hughes's poem seems to assert not only that black people were present in Egypt but also that they built the pyramids: "I looked upon the Nile and raised the pyramids above it." While a reader may initially think of the pyramids having been built through slave labor, whether Hebrew or black, the text of the poem says nothing to suggest that coercion was involved and even hints that the speaker occupies a position of tremendous power, perhaps even the godlike position of pharaoh, and thus can lay claim to the construction of the pyramids as a personal achievement. Afrocentrism often argues this very point, claiming that ancient Egypt was a black civilization and that it, not ancient Greece, was the true source of Western knowledge. For primary source material on Afrocentrism, look for books by leading figures of this school of thought, including Molefi Asante, Yosef Ben-Jochannan, John H. Clarke, and Maulana Karenga. Be advised that Afrocentrism is sharply criticized in both the scholarly and popular presses for alleged oversimplification, misrepresentation, and even implicit racism. Some of the best-known critics include Amy J. Binder, Stephen Howe, Mary Lefkowitz, and Clarence Earl Walker. For example, Walker uses the term *therapeutic mythology* to describe what he sees as the drive of an oppressed group to create new and enabling pasts, even if these pasts remain wholly or partially fictional. In your essay, attempt to connect your discussion of Afrocentrism to the ideas and images presented in Hughes's poem. For example, if you find yourself drawn to Walker's position, consider whether Hughes might be constructing a "therapeutic mythology" of his own in the poem "The Negro Speaks of Rivers."

Compare and Contrast Essays

Sample Topics:

1. **Visual and musical adaptations:** The poem "The Negro Speaks of Rivers" has inspired a number of visual and musical adaptations, many of which were completed with Hughes's direct approval. One or more of these adaptations can be compared and contrasted with the original poem to produce a strong and creative essay that explores more than one medium of artistic expression.

Aaron Douglass's inspired 1941 illustration of Hughes's poem provides ample material for comparison and contrast. The illustration can be found online (in a slightly cropped version) on the website of the Walter O. Evans Collection of African American Art, Heckscher Museum of Art. A smaller but more complete image can be found elsewhere online, such as on the website of the Detroit Institute of Arts. (See the entries pertaining to Aaron Douglass listed at the end of this chapter.) Douglass also illustrated poetic works by other black writers of his time, including James Weldon Johnson's "God's Trombones: Seven Negro Sermons in Verse," but he is probably best known for his murals, journal covers, and other illustrations. You can develop a careful comparison and contrast between Hughes's poem and Douglass's illustration in particular or, more generally, between the shared themes and interests of the two artists, including their focus on working-class blacks, their ideas of a black Egypt, and their strong interest in black history in the New World. Writing about musical adaptations of the poem by Margaret Bonds, Howard Swanson, or others may prove more challenging, but this topic can make for an interesting and creative essay or other academic project. For the sheet music to the composition by Margaret Bonds, see the entry "Music of Social Change" listed at the end of this chapter.

2. **Hughes's "Negroes":** Compare the poem "The Negro Speaks of Rivers" with another short poem from his early career, "Negro" (originally published under the title "Proem").

The third stanza of "Negro" illustrates some of the possible similarities between this poem and "The Negro Speaks of Rivers":

> I've been a worker.
> Under my hand the pyramids arose.
> I made mortar for the Woolworth Building. (lines 7–9)

Among the meaningful similarities that you can discuss are the important role of the first-person speaker, the treatment of history and the passage of time, and the connections that are made between very different continents and civilizations. The other sections of "Negro" will present you with the opportunity to examine the meaningful differences between the poems, such as the presence or absence of racially motivated violence. After reviewing the two poems and learning more about what Hughes knew or did not know about Africa at the time that he wrote these texts, you may wish to explore the question of whether Hughes is talking about a real Africa or a mythical, imaginary one. For example, a later line in the poem, "Negro"—"The Belgians cut off my hands in the Congo"—probably comes not from any intimate knowledge of the history of Africa but rather from general reading or even from fictional works such as Joseph Conrad's *Heart of Darkness*. Rampersad's biography of the poet contains the dates of and detailed information on Hughes's first trip to Africa, as does the first volume of Hughes's autobiography, *The Big Sea*.

3. **Free verse and democratic vistas:** Compare the poem "The Negro Speaks of Rivers" or other poems by Hughes to one or more poems by Walt Whitman or Carl Sandburg, both of whom had very strong influence on the form and content of Hughes's poetry.

You may find similarities between these three poets—Whitman, Sandburg, and Hughes—in specific elements, such as the use of free verse or the emphasis on the everyday activities of people. Or you may find more general similarities in their poetic vision, including their expression of values that are often associated with the literary period of Romanticism. A final parallel between Whitman and Hughes may be the scandal that both caused with the publication of their best-known volumes of verse, *Leaves of Grass* and *Fine Clothes to the Jew*, respectively.

Bibliography and Online Resources for "The Negro Speaks of Rivers"

Ako, Edward O. "Langston Hughes and the Negritude Movement: A Study in Literary Influence." *College Language Association Journal* 28 (1983–84): 46–56.

Arnold, A. James. *Modernism and Negritude: The Poetry and Poetics of Aimé Césaire.* Cambridge: Harvard UP, 1981.

Asante, Molefi K. *Egypt vs. Greece and the American Academy: The Debate over the Birth of Civilization.* Chicago: African American Images, 2002.

Asante, Molefi K. *Afrocentricity: The Theory of Social Change.* Rev. ed. Trenton, N.J.: Africa World P, 1988.

Bâ, Sylvia Washington. *The Concept of Negritude in the Poetry of Léopold Sédar Senghor.* Princeton, N.J.: Princeton UP, 1973.

Binder, Amy J. *Contentious Curricula: Afrocentrism and Creationism in American Public Schools.* Princeton, N.J.: Princeton UP, 2002.

Douglass, Aaron. *The Negro Speaks of Rivers (For Langston Hughes).* 1941. The Detroit Institute of Arts. Available online. URL: http://www.dia.org/exhibitions/woe/preview3.asp. Downloaded on March 3, 2009.

——. *The Negro Speaks of Rivers (For Langston Hughes)*. 1941. The Walter O. Evans Collection of African American Art. Heckscher Museum of Art. Available online. URL: http://eev.liu.edu/eevillage/HeckscherWOE/exhibit9. htm. Downloaded on March 3, 2009.

DuPlessis, Rachel Blau. *Genders, Races, and Religious Cultures in Modern American Poetry, 1908–1934*. New York: Cambridge UP, 2001.

Howe, Stephen. *Afrocentrism: Mythical Pasts and Imagined Homes*. New York: Verso, 1998.

Hughes, Langston. *The Big Sea*. 1940. *The Collected Works of Langston Hughes*. Ed. Joseph McLaren. Vol. 13. Columbia: University of Missouri Press, 2002.

——. "The Negro Speaks of Rivers." *The Dream Keeper and Other Poems*. Folkways Records, 1955. Available online at The Poetry Archive. URL: http://www.poetryarchive.org/poetryarchive/singlePoem.do?poemId=1553. Downloaded on March 3, 2009.

——. "The Negro Speaks of Rivers." *Langston Hughes Reads: One Way Ticket, the Negro Speaks of Rivers, the Klu Klux Klan and Other of His Poems*. HarperCollins, 1992. Available online at Salon.com Audio. URL: http://archive. salon.com/audio/poetry/2001/02/15/langston_hughes/index. Downloaded on March 3, 2009.

——. "The Negro Speaks of Rivers." *The Voice of Langston Hughes*. Smithsonian Folkways Recordings. 1995. Available online at www.poets.org. URL: http://www.poets.org/viewmedia.php/prmMID/15722. Downloaded on March 3, 2009.

——. *Poems from Black Africa: Ethiopia, South Rhodesia, Sierra Leone, Madagascar, Ivory Coast, Nigeria, Kenya, Gabon, Senegal, Nyasaland, Mozambique, South Africa, Congo, Ghana, Liberia*. Bloomington: Indiana UP, 1963.

Hutchinson, George. *The Harlem Renaissance in Black and White*. Cambridge: Harvard UP, 1995.

Jemie, Onwuchekwa. *Langston Hughes: An Introduction to the Poetry*. New York: Columbia UP, 1976.

Joyce, Joyce A. "Bantu, Nkodi, Ndungu, and Nganga: Language, Politics, Music, and Religion in African American Poetry." *The Furious Flowering of African American Poetry*. Ed. Joanne V. Gabbin. Charlottesville: U of Virginia P, 1999. 99–117.

Kim, Daniel Won-gu. "'We, Too, Rise with You': Recovering Langston Hughes' African (Re)Turn 1954–1960 in *An African Treasury*, the *Chicago Defender*, and *Black Orpheus*." *African American Review* 41.3 (2007): 419–41.

Lefkowitz, Mary. *Not Out of Africa: How Afrocentrism Became an Excuse to Teach Myth as History*. New York: Basic Books, 1996.

McCaskill, Barbara. *Post-bellum, Pre-Harlem: African American Literature and Culture, 1877–1919*. New York: New York UP, 2006.

Masolo, D. A. *African Philosophy in Search of Identity*. Bloomington: Indiana UP, 1994.

Mullen, Edward J. *Langston Hughes in the Hispanic World and Haiti*. Hamden: Archon, 1977.

"Music of Social Change: Hughes and 'The Negro Speaks of Rivers.'" Institute of Museum and Library Services and Emory University. Available online. URL: http://www.metascholar.org/MOSC/essays/hughes.htm. Downloaded on March 3, 2009.

"On 'The Negro Speaks of Rivers.'" Modern American Poetry: An Online Journal and Multimedia Companion to *Anthology of Modern American Poetry*. Ed. Cary Nelson. Available online. URL: http://www.english.illinois.edu/maps/poets/g_l/hughes/rivers.htm. Downloaded on March 3, 2009.

Patterson, Anita Haya. *Race, American Literature and Transnational Modernisms*. New York: Cambridge UP, 2008.

Thomas, Lorenzo. "'It Is the Same Everywhere for Me': Langston Hughes and the African Diaspora's Everyman." *Montage of a Dream: The Art and Life of Langston Hughes*. Ed. John Edgar Tidwell, Arnold Rampersad, and Cheryl R. Ragar. Columbia: U of Missouri P, 2007. 181–94.

Vzamane, Mbuelelo Vizikhung. "Apartheid Defines the Contours of American Literary Studies in Southern Africa." *As Others Read Us: International Perspectives on American Literature*. Ed. Huck Gutman. Amherst: U of Massachusetts P, 1991. 219–35.

Wagner, Jean. *Black Poets of the United States: From Paul Laurence Dunbar to Langston Hughes*. Trans. Kenneth Douglass. Urbana: U of Illinois P, 1973.

Walker, Clarence Earl. *We Can't Go Home Again: An Argument about Afrocentrism*. New York: Oxford UP, 2001.

"THE WEARY BLUES"

READING TO WRITE

FIRST PUBLISHED in 1925 in *Opportunity*, the literary and cultural organ of the National Association for the Advancement of Colored People (NAACP), Hughes's poem "The Weary Blues" is often praised for its integration of two different poetic traditions, one using standard English and highly structured, rhymed stanzas, the other employing black vernacular English and blues rhythms. The poem's importance to Hughes's early career can be seen in his use of the poem's title as the title of his first volume of poetry, published in 1926.

Steven Tracy writes in the introduction to his study *Langston Hughes and the Blues* that—like a few of his black contemporaries, including Zora Neale Hurston, James Weldon Johnson, and Sterling Brown—Hughes viewed the blues as "a form of folk poetry" and saw it as something worthy of study, preservation, and even imitation or integration in more formal literature, including his published poems, short stories, and novels (2). As these contemporary artists and later critics have often noted, many educated middle-class blacks in the early 20th century had a different opinion of the blues, considering the genre of music to be low and common, even vulgar, and something more likely to work against rather than work toward the gradual improvement in the status of black Americans. Although the success that Hughes had in placing his book with a large and respected white publisher secured his national status as a promising young poet, his subject matter frequently caused many of his educated black readers to pause and, particularly in his second volume, to question whether what he was presenting in his poems had any social or artistic value.

To formulate an insightful assessment of the work, begin with a close, active reading of the poem—a process that is worthwhile but takes time, attention, and more than one reading. Read for comprehension first. In your second and later readings, record your comments and reactions. Ask questions and make observations about themes and language, perhaps beginning with the difference between the largely conventional poetic frame and the quoted blues lyrics (lines 19–22 and 25–30) contained by that frame. Unlike in the blues poems in his second volume of poetry, Hughes does not present blues lyrics in "The Weary Blues" without a mediator of some kind; here, the blues lyrics are placed within a larger frame. Someone observes, comments on, and quotes the musician as he plays and sings. Does this framing hint at Hughes's desire to remain distant from his subject of the blues? Or does the use of a frame at the beginning of the poem allow Hughes to create distance only to destroy it as the poem progresses? If so, how does the distance collapse toward the end of the poem? You may notice, for example, how the observer is no longer mentioned at the poem's end; the observer and the reader have essentially lost their outsider status and followed the musician home. What could this collapse indicate? Can we take it as a sign that Hughes would encourage the reader to see past the divisions of high and low culture and to see blues lyrics as deserving of the same high status usually granted to formal poetry?

Read the poem aloud at least once to get a better sense of the sounds and patterns in the poem, paying particular attention to alliteration, for example, as well as changes in both form and tone between the framing poem and the embedded blues lyrics. Ask questions as you move through the poem, and make a note of anything that stands out. You may notice, for example, that the opening line contains what is often called a dangling or misplaced modifier—does the present participial phrase "Droning a drowsy syncopated tune" modify the noun "I" or the noun "a Negro" in the clause that follows: "I heard a Negro play. . ."? This observation may be more than simply an exercise in grammar. It may point to how, already in the first line, the poem seeks to collapse the distance between the person who is listening to the blues and the person who is playing them.

In comparison with most of Hughes's poems, "The Weary Blues" is a long poem that makes use of a sophisticated structure and broad vocabulary. Even so, after carefully discussing related elements in the poem, you may have difficulty writing an essay of more than a few pages in length unless you bring in additional, relevant material. Close reading is a good place to begin, but often it is not the place where you will want to end. Review the different topics and strategies in the following section for ideas on how you might develop your essay more fully.

TOPICS AND STRATEGIES
History and Context

Sample Topics:

1. **Structure, history, and meaning of the blues:** Use the incorporation of blues lyrics in the poem "The Weary Blues" as an opportunity to research and discuss the structure, history, and/ or meaning of blues music.

You may choose to begin drafting your essay on Hughes's poem in particular and the blues in general by identifying and defining the eight-bar and twelve-bar blues line, using the lyrics from the poem as your examples. You may want to incorporate Hughes's own concise definition of the blues stanza in the opening of his second volume, *Fine Clothes to the Jew:*

> The *Blues,* unlike the *Spirituals,* have a strict poetic pattern: one long line repeated and a third line to rhyme with the first two. Sometimes the second line in repetition is slightly changed and sometimes, but very seldom, is omitted. The mood of the *Blues* is almost always despondency, but when they are sung people laugh. (73)

You may also find it useful to review the history of the blues in general while remembering to focus specifically on how, as part of the Great Migration northward, blues music made its way from its birthplace to Lenox Avenue, the New York City street named in the poem. Finally, you may wish to explore the cultural meanings of the blues, including the idea of "laughing to keep from crying," an idea stated in the final sentence of the introduction to Hughes's second volume of poetry and used in the title of his 1952 collection of short stories. While writing this essay, take care not to lose sight of your focus on Hughes's poem "The Weary Blues." Steven C. Tracy's book *Langston Hughes and the Blues* may prove to be a valuable resource for an essay on this topic.

2. **Class divisions among African Americans:** Use the criticisms that Hughes received for his focus on the speech, mannerisms, and cultural productions of lower-class blacks as an opportunity to explore the social divisions among black Americans in the early 20th century. Focus on the poem "The Weary Blues" or other relevant works by Hughes.

You may find it helpful to read reviews of Hughes's volumes of poetry, particularly *Fine Clothes to the Jew,* by readers in his own time. A good sample of these reviews and a long introductory essay are presented in Tish Dace's book *Langston Hughes: The Contemporary Reviews.* You may also wish to read W.E.B. Du Bois's essay "The Criteria of Negro Art" or the encyclopedia entry listed at the end of this chapter that discusses the questions and answers appearing in Du Bois's forum in *The Crisis* titled "The Negro in Art—How Shall He Be Portrayed?" In reviewing these items by Du Bois, you may want to pay particular attention to Du Bois's emphasis on the value of art (provided it follow certain standards) in improving the status of African Americans. If you have difficulty locating contemporary reviews of Hughes's poetry, you may find yourself employing Du Bois's position and perhaps seeing Hughes's essay "These Bad Negroes: A Critique on Critics" (1927) as more or less reflecting—or, in Hughes's case, responding to—the views of the well-educated, politically active, socially conscious, middle- or upper-class African American in the first few decades of the 20th century.

Compare and Contrast Essays

Sample Topics:

1. **Distance between Hughes's poetry and the art of "ordinary" blacks:** Explore the ways in which Hughes's poem "The Weary Blues" differs from the blues poems in his second volume of

poetry, *Fine Clothes to the Jew,* perhaps focusing specifically on "Suicide" or "Po' Boy Blues."

Arnold Rampersad asserts that many of Hughes's poems written in the early 1920s offer "the barely mediated recording of the sounds and sights of black life." Rampersad goes on to write:

> In his willingness to stand back and record, with minimal intervention, aspects of the drama of black religion (and, later, of music and dance), Hughes clearly showed that he had begun to see his own learned poetic art, even with his individual talent, as inferior to that of "ordinary" blacks—inferior, for example, to an old black woman in the amen corner who cries to Jesus, "Glory! Hallelujah!" At the heart of his sense of inferiority—which empowered rather than debilitated Hughes—was the knowledge that he (and other would-be poets) stood to a great extent outside the culture he worshipped. Perhaps Hughes stood at a greater distance from the masses than did most other black poets. (qtd. in Bloom, *Langston Hughes: Comprehensive Research and Study Guide,* 61)

In your essay, you will want to keep in mind (and consider quoting some or all of) this statement by Rampersad. Consider focusing on one particular way in which "The Weary Blues" differs from the blues poems in *Fine Clothes to the Jew:* it places the vernacular of the blues lyrics within a frame of standard English rather than presenting them "barely mediated"—that is, more directly and unframed—to the reader of the poem. Use a good dictionary to look up any important terms that might seem a little unfamiliar (such as *mediated*), and strategically repeat Rampersad's terms—remembering to cite him the first time that you use one of his terms—to lend coherence to your essay. Toward the end of your essay, you may wish to comment on which approach—the heavily mediated or the "barely mediated"—seems to you the more successful or appealing of the two, or you may wish to explain how one approach may have been more acceptable than the other to Hughes's middle-class readers.

2. **Variety of stanzas, speakers, subjects, and literary effects:**
   Review at least four poems from each of Hughes's first two collections, *The Weary Blues* and *Fine Clothes to the Jew*. Compare and contrast some or all of the poems in terms of the variety of stanzas, speakers, subjects, and literary effects.

Developing the ideas from a statement by Hughes, Steven Tracy asserts the following on the topic of the differences between Hughes's first two published volumes of poetry: "*Fine Clothes [to the Jew]* was an advance over the blues poems of *The Weary Blues* because of its greater variety of stanzas, speakers, subjects, and literary effects" (4). Explore whether or not you find yourself agreeing with Tracy's general assertion that the poems included in the second volume show a greater range in form, content, and technique than the poems included in the first volume. R. Baxter Miller's *The Art and Imagination of Langston Hughes* may offer a countering view, with its discussion of the range of themes and techniques in *The Weary Blues*. Each poem that you choose to focus on can receive a short, close reading in your essay; of course, the level of detail in each close reading will be determined by the total number of poems and the length of the essay that you are writing.

3. **Religious views:** Explore how, in "The Weary Blues" and in a number of other poems, Hughes uses musical performances as a way of metaphorically talking about his views on life, death, and the afterlife (or the absence of an afterlife).

In a number of poems in his first two volumes of poetry, including "The Weary Blues," "Sport," and "Saturday Night," Hughes uses musical performances or cabarets and the people who frequent them as a way of metaphorically talking about his views on life and mortality. You may note, for example, that these poems show places and people full of frenetic energy and motion for a short time, then suddenly falling silent as the poems end.

Bibliography for "The Weary Blues"

Dace, Tish. *Langston Hughes: The Contemporary Reviews.* New York: Cambridge UP, 1997.

Kelley, James. "The Crisis: The Negro in Art—How Shall He Be Portrayed? A Symposium." *Encyclopedia of the Harlem Renaissance.* Vol. 1. Ed. Cary D. Wintz and Paul Finkelman. New York: Routledge, 2004. 267–68.

Miller, R. Baxter. *The Art and Imagination of Langston Hughes.* Lexington: UP of Kentucky, 1986.

Rampersad, Arnold. "Langston Hughes' *Fine Clothes to the Jew.*" *Callaloo* 9 (1986). Rpt. *Langston Hughes.* Ed. Harold Bloom. Broomall, Penn.: Chelsea House, 1999. 60–61.

Tracy, Steven C. *Langston Hughes and the Blues.* 1985. Urbana: U of Illinois P, 2001.

"I, TOO"

READING TO WRITE

THE POEM known today as "I, Too" originally appeared under the title "Epilogue" and was the final statement made by Hughes in his first volume of poetry, *The Weary Blues*, which was published in 1926. In nearly all of the countless reprintings and discussions of this poem—including in textbooks, anthologies, and analyses—editors and critics have followed Hughes's lead by replacing the original title with the first words of the poem.

Already in the two simple, direct statements that open the poem—"I, too, sing America. / I am the darker brother"—Hughes expresses a complex topic: the tension between being both an American citizen and a black person in the early decades of the 20th century. This black American, for example, would have been by definition a member of a great democratic experiment yet would also frequently have been denied the basic rights that go along with that membership. Thus, Hughes's poem might been seen as an expression of what W.E.B. Du Bois has called *double-consciousness*, as he defines the term in his influential collection of essays, *The Souls of Black Folk:*

It is a peculiar sensation, this double-consciousness, this sense of always looking at oneself through the eyes of others, of measuring one's soul by the tape of a world that looks on in amused contempt and pity. One ever feels his twoness—an American, a Negro; two souls, two thoughts, two unreconciled strivings; two warring ideals in one body, whose dogged strength alone keeps it from being torn asunder.

Much like a black person possessing the double-consciousness described by Du Bois, Hughes's poem seems to be at war with itself, and the speaker in the poem seems to be pulled in two directions at once. He laughs at his marginal social status in the second stanza of the poem, but he also has aggressive thoughts in the stanza that follows about how "[n]obody'll dare" continue to marginalize him (line 11). Similarly, the speaker claims to possess two contradictory characteristics that, in the near future, will contribute to his full rights no longer being denied: He possesses both strength and beauty. The poem implies that the first characteristic, strength, will intimidate white people into changing their ways, whereas the second, beauty, will make them feel "ashamed" (line 17) of their mistreatment of him.

To formulate a strong approach to an essay on this work, begin with a close, active reading of the poem. Read for comprehension first. In your second and later readings, record your comments and reactions. Read the poem aloud at least once to get a better sense of the rhythms and music of the lines. Isolate important phrases, repeated words, and related images that you feel will bolster your argument.

Ask questions, and make observations about themes and language, perhaps beginning with the first two words of the poem. The words "I, too" suggest that he is not alone in doing what he does. Someone else also "sing[s] America" or has sung America before him. Exactly who this is, though, is never clearly stated in the poem. You might be interested in exploring the possibilities. A number of readers have speculated that the poem "I Hear America Singing" in Walt Whitman's *Leaves of Grass* is referenced here, as detailed in one of the possible topics suggested in this chapter. These words "I, too, sing America" also assert participation in a creative act, an assertion that counters the speaker's marginalized position in the poem.

In your close reading, you may want to reflect on the "darker brother" (line 2) and on the poem's sustained focus on a domestic setting, perhaps even on a single-family home with a dining room (where the guests are entertained) and a separate kitchen (where the meals are prepared). What sort of kinship is the speaker asserting with the family in this home when he says "I am the darker brother"? Is it more likely a literal or a figurative kinship? Does it matter whether you believe the speaker is addressing a family or other group that is white or one that is black?

Continuing along this line of inquiry, you might reflect on the personal pronoun "they," used twice in the poem without an antecedent, a noun to which a pronoun usually refers and replaces. Who is this undefined group of people? Are "they" the other family members or some entirely different group of people? Do the absence of a clear antecedent and the repetition of the word *they* suggest something about the speaker's level of intimacy with this group of people?

You may also want to look closely at the stanza divisions in the poem and explore possible connections between the poem's form and its meaning. Do the divisions in the poem seem random, or does some pattern emerge when you consider them more closely? Are ideas developed in a certain order in the poem? When reading any poem, you may want to pay particular attention to repeated words or phrases and note, in particular, any instances in the poem of repetition with variation. What is the effect of the repeated line "When company comes," for example? How do you make sense of the transformation of "I, too, sing America" in the opening line to "I, too, am America" in the final line? How do these repetitions establish connections between the stanzas?

TOPICS AND STRATEGIES
Philosophy and Ideas

Sample Topics:

1. **Walt Whitman and Langston Hughes:** Explore the possible influence or inspiration of Walt Whitman on Hughes in general and the possible influence of the poem "I Hear America Singing" on the poem "I, Too" in particular.

Arnold Rampersad writes in his biography that the poem "I, Too" by Hughes "depart[s] from Whitman's celebrated chant" and expresses the poet's "unhappy mood" (95). Read Whitman's poem "I Hear America Singing" and consider whether it is likely, for example, that Hughes is seeking as a black poet to join the melody of laborers while calling attention to the racial diversity that makes up his America. You may want to use the indexes in Berry's and Rampersad's biographies of Hughes to locate references to Whitman. In your essay, you may want to discuss other, more general connections between Whitman and Hughes.

2. **Ways of securing racial equality:** Explore the possible treatment of the two or more ways of securing racial equality in the poem "I, Too."

The poem "I, Too" hints that there may be more than one way of getting what one wants. The speaker suggests that gaining the physical power to impose one's will may be one way but ends the poem with the hope that the use of strength will be unnecessary. This idea of having several ways to secure racial equality might be applied to the struggles for black equality in the 1950s and early 1960s. Alongside the affirming speeches and the courageous nonviolent resistance of heroes such as Rosa Parks and Martin Luther King Jr. were the very real threats and all-too-clear instances of civil unrest and urban riots. Hughes's poem may provide you with an opportunity to expand your understanding of this complex and frequently oversimplified element of the civil rights era. To begin, you may wish to consult Lance Hill's book *The Deacons for Defense: Armed Resistance and the Civil Rights Movement.*

3. **Changes to the poem:** Reflect on the possible significance of a seemingly small change that Hughes made to the poem "I, Too" later in his career. The line "They'll see how beautiful I am" was changed in later presentations of the poem to read, "They'll see how beautiful we are."

In addition to the change in title Hughes eventually made to his poem, you may notice this second change when you listen to the 1955 Smithsonian Folkways recording and read the transcribed text of that recording against the original 1926 poem: the "I am" at the end of the line has been changed to "we are." You may also find it significant that Hughes, in introducing the poem in this recording, speaks not about a single person but rather about "a whole race of people" and "the Negro people." Consider exploring how this poem can be read to be more than expressing an individual's longing to be a fully valued member of his own family. The small changes to the poem might reflect the beginnings, already in the 1950s, of dramatic changes in race relations in the United States. Perhaps consider what sorts of activities for securing racial equality were under way in or around 1955.

4. **Double-consciousness:** Explore how Hughes's poem "I, Too" embodies some of the tensions identified by W.E.B. Du Bois in his definition of double-consciousness.

Review the excerpt from Du Bois's *The Souls of Black Folk* provided previously in this chapter and explore the connections between his idea of double-consciousness and Hughes's poem "I, Too." Focus on the split or tension that Du Bois identifies between being American and being black at the beginning of the 20th century: "One ever feels his twoness—an American, a Negro; two souls. . . ." You may want to read and include in your discussion a second poem by Hughes, "Let American Be America Again," which may also address this difficulty of being both American and black. You may find it helpful to learn more about the particular status of African Americans in the first few decades of the 20th century and to use that information to explain in your essay why African Americans in the early 20th century might have felt that split or tension more acutely than African Americans today. Locate a few solid resources on black life in the segregation era, such as Marlon Bryan Ross's *Manning the Race: Reforming Black Men in the Jim Crow Era* or Glenda Elizabeth Gilmore's *Gender and Jim Crow: Women and the Politics of White Supremacy in North Carolina, 1896–1920.*

5. **The "struggle to achieve full citizenship":** Explore how the poem "I, Too" (as well as perhaps other works by Hughes) embodies what Richard K. Barksdale sees as the dominant theme in Hughes's writings: the black "struggle to achieve full citizenship" (x).

Hughes's poem "I, Too" has perhaps the clearest articulation of this central theme identified by Barksdale, but in exploring other works by Hughes, you are likely to encounter the same theme again and again. You may want to look at some of Hughes's other poems (such as "Let America Be America Again"), short stories (such as "The Blues I'm Playing"), or novels (such as *Not Without Laughter*). In analyzing two or more of Hughes's works, you may find subtle differences in the treatment of this theme over the course of his career.

Bibliography and Online Resources for "I, Too"

Barksdale, Richard K. *Langston Hughes: The Poet and His Critics.* Chicago: American Library, 1977.

Du Bois, W.E.B. *The Souls of Black Folk.* Eds. Henry Louis Gates, Jr. and Terri Hume Oliver. New York: W.W. Norton, 1999.

Hughes, Langston. "I, Too." *The Dream Keeper and Other Poems.* Folkways Records, 1955. Available online at The Poetry Archive. URL: http://www.poetry archive.org/poetryarchive/singlePoem.do?poemId=1552. Downloaded on March 3, 2009.

Hill, Lance. *The Deacons for Defense: Armed Resistance and the Civil Rights Movement.* Chapel Hill: U of North Carolina P, 2004.

Whitman. Walt. *Leaves of Grass.* Ed. Jerome Loving. New York: Oxford UP, 2009.

Rampersad, Arnold. *The Life of Langston Hughes. Vol. 1: 1902–1941. I, Too, Sing America.* 2nd edition. New York: Oxford UP, 2002.

"SONG FOR
A DARK GIRL"

READING TO WRITE

THE POEM "Song for a Dark Girl" was included in Hughes's second volume, *Fine Clothes to the Jew*, published in 1927, and has since been widely anthologized. Although very short, the poem does not lack scope or resonance and is likely to provide any number of starting points for a strong essay.

Consider the title of the poem. Is the "Dark Girl" mentioned in the title also the person speaking the poem, or is she the person being spoken about? In other words, is she the mourner of the person lynched or the victim of the lynching? Many of Hughes's contemporary readers and many of the later critics take the girl to be the speaker of the lines in the poem, lamenting the death of her lynched male lover, but at least two sources read the poem as "represent[ing] . . . a young black woman's lynching" (Pozorski 716) or dealing with "premature death, aborted life, represented by a young black woman" (Clarke 88). Do the title and the details (or lack of details) about the speaker and victim in Hughes's poem allow for both readings? Do you tend to find one reading stronger or more compelling than the other? Or are you, as a reader, willing to entertain both possibilities and perhaps even others?

As you progress in your reading of the poem, you may make note of certain phrases or patterns that stand out. You may view the recurring line "Way down south in Dixie"—which appears three times in the short poem and begins every stanza—as important to your understanding of the poem. A number of people writing about and responding to the poem (whether implicitly or explicitly) address that line and attempt to identify its origins. At least two sources identify call-and-response patterns (Ferguson 95, Hill 165) and another source mentions the spirituals (Fabre 240), but most critics who present an extended discussion of this poem identify the source of the recurring phrase in the poem as having its origins in the famous song "Dixie." These critics also often focus, quite rightly, on the bizarre juxtaposition of lyrics from this unofficial anthem of the Confederacy, which tells about a former black slave longing to return to the plantation where he was born, with the poem's subject of brutal lynching.

In *Poetry of Mourning: The Modern Elegy from Hardy to Heaney,* Jahan Ramazani offers one of the most extensive analyses of the poem and pairs "Song for a Dark Girl" with several other poems by Hughes and other African-American writers of the 20th century. Ramazani argues that "Song for a Dark Girl" belongs to a subgenre of Hughes's elegiac verse, which he calls "the lynch poem." He goes on to list other writers and works that fit within this tradition. It is, he writes, "a subgenre that encompasses such works as Claude McKay's 'The Lynching,' [Countee] Cullen's 'The Black Christ,' and the Lewis Allan poem famously rendered by Billie Holiday, 'Strange Fruit'" (167) as well as two later poems, Gwendolyn Brooks's "The Last Quatrain of the Ballad of Emmett Till" (published in 1960) and Robert Hayden's "Night, Death, Mississippi" (published in 1966). You may be interested in reading "Song for a Dark Girl" against any or all of these works, or you may be interested in reading the poem against three other poems that were written by Hughes and that are also analyzed in Ramazani's study: "Silhouette" (1929), "Blue Bayou" (1943), and "The Bitter River" (1943). After giving each poem careful attention, Ramazani makes generalizing statements about the grouping as a whole, writing that these four poems constitute "the cycle of Hughes' lynch elegies, each one longer than the last, and each one shifting in its primary perspective, from mourner to lyncher to victim and now to the collective voice of the poet" (169–70).

Of course, Ramazani quite rightly does not attempt to address all of Hughes's poems that mention or depict lynching, and you may be interested in reading other poems by Hughes that deal with this subject. In doing so, perhaps you may find yourself in a position to test Ramazani's formulation of "the cycle of Hughes' lynch elegies" by asking any number of related questions. For example, which poems does he leave out of this cycle? Would the inclusion of these poems strengthen, modify, or challenge this notion of a cycle? Do you see another way of grouping and making sense of Hughes's poems on lynching? You may want to look at any or all of the following poems by Hughes that make reference to lynching but are not discussed by Ramazani.

Volume one of *The Collected Works of Langston Hughes* includes no fewer than five such poems. The eight-line poem "Flight" in *Dear Lovely Death* (1931) tells, in condensed form, the story of black man who is suspected of assaulting a white woman and is on the run from a lynch mob. In addition to the fifteen-line poem "Lynching Song," Hughes's 1938 collection of poems, *A New Song*, contains a number of poems that make brief references to lynching: The poem "A New Song" reflects on a time when "the lyncher's rope / Hung about my neck" and "the fire scorched my feet" (lines 18–19, 20), the poem "Open Letter to the South" mentions a "lynching tree" (line 44), and the uncollected poem "One More 'S' in the U.S.A." has two lines about the subject: "But we can't join hands together / So long as whites are lynching black" (lines 26–27).

Similarly, volume two of *The Collected Works of Langston Hughes* includes no fewer than five such poems. In the volume *Shakespeare in Harlem* (1942), the poem "Southern Mammy Sings" has at least one full stanza on lynching, whereas among the generally more radical poems in *Jim Crow's Last Stand* (1943), several take up the subject to varying degrees, including at least one short poem not discussed by Ramazani, "Freedom." At least two additional poems on lynching appear in the volume *One Way Ticket* (1949), "Lynching Song" and "One Way Ticket." Among the uncollected poems is a reference to lynching in "Madam and the Newsboy."

Finally, volume three of *The Collected Works of Langston Hughes* includes no fewer than six such poems. At least two poems on lynching appear in *The Panther and the Lash* (1967), but in these poems the treatment of lynching may be seen as more metaphorical than it is in most or all of the previous poems: "Death in Yorkville" likens the 1964 police shooting of a young black man to a lynching, and a second poem—"Christ in Alabama"—suggests a parallel between the Crucifixion of Christ and the lynching of blacks. Other poems in volume three that treat the subject of lynching include "A Ballad of Negro History," "Ballad of Walter White," "Song after Lynching," and "Song of Adoration."

As is the case with many of Hughes's poems, "Song for a Dark Girl" is a short poem and uses what might appear to be a simple structure and vocabulary. Thus, even after carefully discussing related elements in the poem, you may have difficulty writing a paper of more than a few pages in length unless you bring in additional relevant material. Close reading is a good place to begin, but often it is not the place where you will want to end. Review the different topics and strategies in the following section for ideas on how you might develop your paper idea more fully.

TOPICS AND STRATEGIES
History and Context

Sample Topics:

1. **Lynching:** Explore the realities of lynching alongside the literary treatment of the same topic by Hughes in the poem "Song for a Dark Girl."

   As discussed in the opening section of this chapter, Hughes wrote a number of poems on lynching. You may wish to analyze one particular poem, consider how a group of Hughes's poems fit together, or perhaps compare Hughes's treatment of lynching with that of one or more other poets. You may wish to focus your discussion on the first half of the 20th century. Hughes also wrote several short stories in which lynching figures prominently, including "Father to Son" and "Home."

2. **Histories and meanings of "Dixie":** Explore the different explanations for the origins of the song "Dixie" and analyze the song's lyrics just as you might analyze a poem. Consider how this new information can enrich your understanding of Hughes's poem "Song for a Dark Girl."

   In researching the history of "Dixie," you may find claims that the song has its origins in the minstrel (blackface) shows of the 1850s and that the song was popular some time before becoming the unofficial anthem of the Confederacy. You may also find that while Dan Emmett is generally credited as the author of the song, at least one scholarly source argues that "Dixie" may have originated with a free black family living in the early 19th century. See the listed books by Hans Nathan and by

Howard and Judith Sacks for more information on the possible origins of the song. Remember to apply this information to your understanding of Hughes's poem. For example, you may want to show in your paper how your more developed knowledge of the possible history and meaning of the song allow you now to identify and to appreciate and discuss the presence and function of irony in the poem "Song for a Dark Girl."

Philosophy and Ideas

Sample Topics:

1. **Religion and race:** Explore the meaning of the statement, easily overlooked in the poem "Song for a Dark Girl," that Jesus is white.

   Reflect on the lines "I asked the white Lord Jesus / What was the use of prayer" (lines 7–8). Explore how and why Jesus might indeed be depicted as white in mainstream American images. If possible, analyze images of Jesus from the early 20th century. To further develop your essay, you might consider exploring the topic of a black Christ, as developed in Hughes's poetry or other writings (see, for example, his poem "Christ in Alabama" or his novel *Tambourines to Glory*), in the poetry of his contemporary Countee Cullen, or in the work of other black artists from any period.

2. **The use of prayer:** Analyze Hughes's treatment in the poem "Song for a Dark Girl" and elsewhere in his poetry or other writings of the subject of religion, prayer, or perhaps a related but more abstract concept, such as hope, surrender, or salvation.

   Write an essay examining the place of religion or a related concept in Hughes's poetry. Reflect on the lines "I asked the white Lord Jesus / What was the use of prayer" (lines 7–8) in his poem "Song for a Dark Girl." You may want to consider the question in light of Hughes's other poems modeled on spontaneous prayers, sermons, and other manifestations of popular black Christianity. See, for example, the cluster of nine poems grouped under "Glory! Hallelujah!" in his second volume of poetry, *Fine Clothes to the Jew.* Hughes's skepticism or at least ambivalence toward organized religion may be seen, too, in a number of his short stories (see, for example, "Father and Son," "On the Road," "Big Meeting," and "Rock, Church") as well as in his second novel, *Tambourines to Glory.*

Compare and Contrast Essays

Sample Topics:

1. **Metaphors of love:** Compare and contrast the poem "Song for a Dark Girl" with the poem "Love Song for Lucinda" or other poems by Hughes that address the topic of love through metaphors.

   Consider beginning your analysis by focusing on the figures of speech that are used in the two poems. More specifically, the lines "Love is a naked shadow / On a gnarled and naked tree" ("Song for a Dark Girl," lines 11–12) seem at first a far cry from "Love / Is a ripe plum / Growing on a purple tree" ("Love Song for Lucinda," lines 1–3). You may want to account for the difference in these two figures of speech by explaining the different contexts of the poems in which these lines occur. You may also want to consider if these two poems are really all that different from each other. A second, more careful reading of "Love Song for Lucinda" may reveal that this poem does not present a wholly positive and uncomplicated treatment of love, either. You may also want to address how both poems talk about love without using clichéd phrases or images. A further poem to consider discussing, because it uses a similarly phrased and equally surprising metaphor of love, is Hughes's poem "Beale Street Love," which opens "Love / Is a brown man's fist" (lines 1–2).

2. **Poems against exploitation and abuse:** Compare and contrast the poem "Song for a Dark Girl" and one or more poems by Hughes (or poems by Hughes and one or more other writers) that protest against exploitation and abuse.

   Donald C. Dickinson writes: "Poems like 'Song for a Dark Girl,' 'Bound No'th Blues,' 'Daybreak in Alabama,' and 'Mulatto' all cry out against the southern system of exploitation and abuse" (17). Consider writing an essay that takes Dickinson's grouping as its point of departure and that looks closely at the four poems that he names, combining a brief but close reading of each poem with a more general discussion of what these four works share in common. In a variation of this topic, create and analyze your own grouping of poems by Hughes (or by Hughes and one or more other writers). You will want to include in your essay a clear explanation, like the one given by Dickinson above, of the ways in which the poems that you have grouped are connected. Without this sort of explanation, the grouping may appear random or arbitrary.

3. **Poems about dead black girls:** Compare and contrast the poem "Song for a Dark Girl" and one or more other poems on the subject of African-American women who die before their time. Draw meaningful connections between the poems.

You may wish to use as your starting point Cheryl Clarke's argument that Alice Walker's poem "Ballad of the Brown Girl," published in the volume *Once* in 1969, is "a response to and revision of [Countee] Cullen's 1925 'A Brown Girl Dead' and Hughes' 1927 'Song for a Dark Girl'" (88). First, how similar are Cullen's and Hughes's poems? How might Walker's poem be seen as a response to one or both of them?

Bibliography and Online Resources for "Song for a Dark Girl"

Clarke, Cheryl. *"After Mecca": Women Poets and the Black Arts Movement.* Piscataway, N.J.: Rutgers UP, 2005.

Dickinson, Donald C. *A Bio-bibliography of Langston Hughes, 1902–1967.* 2nd ed. North Haven, Conn.: Archon Books, 1972.

Fabre, Genevieve, and Michel Feith. *Temples for Tomorrow: Looking Back at the Harlem Renaissance.* Bloomington: Indiana UP, 2001.

Ferguson, Jeffrey Brown. *The Harlem Renaissance: A Brief History with Documents.* New York: Macmillan, 2007.

Hill, Patricia Alveda Liggins. *The New Black Aesthetic as a Counterpoetics: The Poetry of Etheridge Knight.* Stanford University, 1977. Abstracted in Dissertation Abstracts International, v. 38A (1977) no. 6, p. 3482-A.

Nathan, Hans (1962). *Dan Emmett and the Rise of Early Negro Minstrelsy.* Norman, Okla.: University of O P, 1962.

Pozorski, Aimee L. "Poetry." In Elizabeth Ann Beaulieu's *Writing African American Women: K–Z.* Westport, Conn.: Greenwood P, 2006. 715–21.

Ramazani, Jahan. *Poetry of Mourning: The Modern Elegy from Hardy to Heaney.* Chicago: U of Chicago P, 1994.

Rice, Anne P. *Witnessing Lynching: American Writers Respond.* Piscataway, N.J.: Rutgers UP, 2003.

Sacks, Howard L., and Judith Rose Sacks. *Way up North in Dixie: A Black Family's Claim to the Confederate Anthem.* Washington, D.C.: Smithsonian Institution P, 1993.

"Without Sanctuary: Photographs and Postcards of Lynching in America." Collection of James Allen and John Littlefield. Available online. URL: http://www.withoutsanctuary.org/main.html. Downloaded on March 3, 2009.

"GOODBYE CHRIST"

READING TO WRITE

HUGHES'S POEM "Goodbye Christ" was published in 1932 in the leftist journal *The Negro Worker* and was reprinted in Nancy Cunard's *Negro: An Anthology* (1934) alongside several of Hughes's other provocative, even radical poems from the early 1930s. Hughes did not include this poem in any of the main volumes of his poetry published in his lifetime, yet the poem did not fade into oblivion.

At least twice in his lifetime, once around 1940 and again in the early 1950s, Hughes was the target of unwanted attention because of this poem and other poems on related themes. Around 1940, as his biographer Arnold Rampersad writes, Hughes was hounded by a Christian evangelical group that was offended because he had named and criticized their leader Aimee Semple McPherson in his poem "Goodbye Christ" (6). In the early 1950s, Hughes was called to testify before the House Un-American Activities Committee and account for the socialist poetry and prose that he had written in the 1930s, including the poem "Goodbye Christ." The "Right-Wing Anti-Hughes Flier," a document that is available online through the Modern American Poetry website and is included in the bibliography and list of online resources at the end of this chapter, captures this fundamentalist and nationalistic reaction to Hughes's poem, demonstrating how extreme religion and extreme patriotism worked side by side to condemn the poet for his more radical verse. Particularly because of the poem's highly charged reception in two different periods in American history, a detailed discussion of "Goodbye Christ" presents the opportunity to explore a wide range of issues and topics.

To formulate a strong approach to an essay on the poem, begin with a close reading of the work. Read for comprehension first. In your second and later readings, record your comments and reactions. Read the poem aloud at least once to get a better sense of the sounds and patterns in the poem. Because this poem is only two pages in length, you may want to print or photocopy it in order to underline or highlight important phrases, repeated words, and related images on your photocopy. Ask questions and make observations about themes and language, perhaps beginning with the title and first two words of the poem. The opening words—"Listen, Christ"— may shock some readers, irrespective of their belief system, because from the onset, the poem addresses a person considered by many to be the physical manifestation of God as someone to be ordered around rudely and ultimately dismissed. You may note that the poem contains a series of other, perhaps even more shocking commands that are also addressed to Christ, including "Beat it on away from here now" (line 19), "Go ahead on now" (line 24), and "Move! / Don't be so slow about movin'!" (lines 32–33).

As you continue in your close reading of the poem, you may first ask and later attempt to answer any number of other questions. For example, why is a Hindu spiritual leader, Gandhi, named alongside the Roman Catholic authority, Pope Pius? Who are Aimee Semple McPherson and George Wilson Becton, and what do the two have in common? Why are all of the nouns in one line capitalized, even those that are not proper nouns: "Marx Communist Lenin Peasant Stalin Worker ME—" (line 22)?

In comparison to most of Hughes's poems, "Goodbye Christ" is relatively long (thirty-seven lines in length) and makes use of a range of historical allusions that may provide you with additional material for discussion in a paper. Even so, after carefully discussing related elements in the poem and identifying the persons named in the poem, you may have difficulty writing a paper of more than a few pages in length unless you bring in additional relevant material. Review the different topics and strategies in the following section for ideas on how you might develop your paper idea more fully.

TOPICS AND STRATEGIES
History and Context

Sample Topics:

1. **1930s radicalism:** Explore how the poem "Goodbye Christ" fits within the trend in the 1930s among many American writers to produce increasingly politicized works.

You may want to explore the reasons for the social radicalism that emerged in the United States in the 1930s, including the economic hardships of the Great Depression and the lasting discrimination against African Americans. This topic can be modified to include a discussion of how and why Hughes personally became more radical as a writer and how and why, around 1940, he mostly stopped writing this sort of openly politicized poetry. You may want to review the biographies of Hughes by Faith Berry and Arnold Rampersad for related information on the poet.

2. **McCarthyism and cold war America:** Explain the reasons why the poem "Goodbye Christ" and other poems by Hughes from the 1930s prompted his being called to testify before McCarthy's House Un-American Activities Committee in 1953.

Review the methods and goals of the House Un-American Activities Committee, particularly as they relate to the strong interest in American artists. You may also wish to address in your essay Hughes's poem "Un-American Investigators" (*The Collected Works of Langston Hughes* 3: 175–76), which potentially reveals Hughes's true feelings toward McCarthy.

Philosophy and Ideas

Sample Topics:

1. **Skepticism toward organized religion:** Explore Hughes's skepticism toward organized religion, as expressed in the poem "Goodbye Christ" or elsewhere in his poetry or other writings.

Establish through your careful reading of "Goodbye Christ" and perhaps a range of Hughes's poems or other writings his skepticism toward Christianity and other organized religions, his pairing of Christian belief systems with exploitation of the working class, and his desire to replace these belief systems with Marxist ideals. In this analysis, you may wish to pair your discussion of "Goodbye Christ" with a second work by Hughes, whether a poem (such as "Brass Spittoons"), a short story (such as "Father and Son"), or a novel (such as *Tambourines to Glory*).

2. Marxism and blacks: Explore the reasons why substantial numbers of African Americans were drawn to socialist and communist ideals in the early to mid-20th century.

Hughes was by no means the only black intellectual to embrace socialist ideas in the 20th century. In examining the extent to which a more radical political slant influenced black writers of the era, consider reviewing the studies by James Smethurst and William J. Maxwell cited at the end of this chapter. When possible, use the poem "Goodbye Christ" or perhaps other writings by Hughes to illustrate your main points.

3. Capitalizing on Christ: Explore the validity of the claim that the speaker in the poem "Goodbye Christ" makes about the Bible and about Christianity in general: "The popes and the preachers've / Made too much money from it. / They've sold you to too many" (lines 7–9).

In writing an essay on this topic, you might draw on cultural and historical studies of Christianity in the early decades of the 20th century, preferably books by university presses or other reputable publishers. Consider devoting at least part of the essay to a discussion of the two evangelical Christian leaders denounced in the poem, Aimee Semple McPherson and George Wilson Becton. For information on McPherson, look for Matthew Avery Sutton's book *Aimee Semple McPherson and the Resurrection of Christian America*. For information on Becton, review Hughes's detailed discussion of him in the "Spectacles in Color" section of *The Big Sea* (210–12) as well as the entry on him in *The Encyclopedia of the Harlem Renaissance*. For a more general discussion of Christianity in early-20th-century America, read the introductory essay and review some of the documents relevant to the time period in Milton Sernett's *African American Religious History: A Documentary Witness*. Alternately, you might use Hughes's poem as an opportunity to examine the commercialization of religion in contemporary American society. A possible source for this topic may be William Connoll's *Capitalism and Christianity, American Style.* A variation on this topic may be to explore what Harold Bloom calls Hughes's "lifelong suspicion of religion" (53), a sentiment presented, among other places, in his later novel *Tambourines to Glory.*

Bibliography and Online Resources for "Goodbye Christ"

"A Right-Wing Anti-Hughes Flier." Modern American Poetry: An Online Journal and Multimedia Companion to *Anthology of Modern American Poetry.* Ed. Cary Nelson. Available online. URL: http://www.english.illinois.edu/maps/poets/g_l/hughes/flier.htm. Downloaded on March 3, 2009.

Bloom, Harold, ed. *Langston Hughes.* Broomall, Penn.: Chelsea House, 1999.

Connoll, William. *Capitalism and Christianity, American Style.* Durham, N.C.: Duke UP, 2008.

Criniti, Steven F. "Becton, George Wilson." *Encyclopedia of the Harlem Renaissance.* Vol. 1. Ed. Cary D. Wintz and Paul Finkelman. New York: Routledge, 2004. 110–12.

Howard, Walter T. *Black Communists Speak on Scottsboro: A Documentary History.* Philadelphia: Temple UP, 2008.

Hughes, Langston. *The Big Sea.* 1940. *The Collected Works of Langston Hughes.* Ed. Joseph McLaren. Vol. 13. Columbia: U of Missouri P, 2002.

Lackey, Michael. *African American Atheists and Political Liberation: A Study of the Sociocultural Dynamics of Faith.* Gainesville: UP of Florida, 2007.

Maxwell, William J. *New Negro, Old Left: African-American Writing and Communism Between the Wars.* New York: Columbia UP, 1999.

Sernett, Milton, ed. and intro. *African American Religious History: A Documentary Witness.* 2nd ed. Durham: Duke University Press, 1999.

Smethurst, James. *The New Red Negro: The Literary Left and African American Poetry, 1930–1946.* New York: Oxford UP, 1999.

Sutton, Matthew Avery. *Aimee Semple McPherson and the Resurrection of Christian America.* Cambridge, Mass.: Harvard UP, 2007.

"BALLAD OF BOOKER T."

READING TO WRITE

WRITTEN IN 1941 but not included in any of the volumes of poetry published in Hughes's lifetime, "Ballad of Booker T." certainly offers a number of opportunities for students seeking a topic for a strong, original essay.

The refrain in Hughes's poem, "Let down your bucket / where you are," is taken almost word for word from the catch phrase in Booker T. Washington's 1895 speech at the Cotton States and International Exposition in Atlanta: "Cast down your bucket where you are." The phrase captures Washington's two-pronged argument that black Americans in the South, only approximately 30 years after the abolition of slavery, would be better served by staying in the blue-collar jobs that they already knew how to do well and indeed learned how to do well because of slavery—including agricultural labor and domestic service—and that white Americans in the South would be better served by employing the black members of their local workforce in favor of employing newly arrived immigrants, whom he calls "those of foreign birth and strange tongue and habits."

As this summary of Washington's argument hopefully suggests, his philosophy of black Americans staying in familiar places and familiar jobs, working hard, and bettering themselves in order to bring about gradual improvement in race relations has been and remains today charged with controversy and elicits strong emotions on both sides of the debate. Washington's contemporary, W.E.B. Du Bois, for example, placed his hopes not in the hard, steady labor of the black working classes but rather in the "Talented Tenth," an educated and elite group of African Americans who he believed would spearhead the drive for racial equality. It is easy to oversimplify the positions of Washington and Du Bois and to overlook both what they share in common and how their differences may be connected to their different geographies and backgrounds. Indeed, when discussing these two black leaders of the late 19th and early 20th centuries, people tend to oversimplify and to praise one at the expense of the other.

Hughes seems to have held strong views in regard to Washington, but as his poems illustrate, these views change dramatically over time. In the poem "Open Letter to the South," published in Hughes's 1938 collection *A New Song*, the speaker announces his audience—"[w]hite workers of the South" (line 1)—and his identity, "I am the black worker" (line 12). In what he says to his audience, the speaker in this poem, like the speaker in "Ballad of Booker T.," adopts a metaphor famously used by Washington and found not in the image of the bucket but in the hand, which Washington used in his writings and speeches to express the idea that racial segregation can exist alongside a greater unity of purpose. The speaker in "Open Letter to the South" rejects outright this metaphor and the continuation of any sort of racial division that the metaphor supports:

> Let us forget what Booker T. said,
> "Separate as the fingers."
>
> Let us become instead, you and I,
> One single hand
> That can united rise
> To smash the old dead dogmas of the past—(lines 19–24)

Three years later, however, Hughes writes "Ballad of Booker T." In this poem, he seems to reverse his position on Washington, describing the black leader as "practical," "nobody's fool," and "far-seeing" (lines 2, 33, 41).

Washington was a topic for Hughes in more than these two poems. A number of other poems written by Hughes make reference—sometimes glancing, sometimes substantial—to Washington and his philosophy of gradualism. Among the "Uncollected Poems, 1921–30" is the poem

"Alabama Earth." It bears the dedication "(At Booker Washington's grave),"
praises "the truth a simple heart has held" (line 7), and seems to share
Washington's vision of the long road ahead: "Serve—and hate will die
unborn. / Love—and chains are broken" (lines 11–12). Included in the later
volume *Jim Crow's Last Stand* (1943) is the poem "To Captain Mulzac,"
with a subtitle naming the ship *The Booker T. Washington* (2. 86–88). The
poem is free of irony in its praise of harmony between the members of the
interracial crew and the white captain of the ship. The volume "Uncollected Poems, 1941–50" contains the poem "Ballad of the Seven Songs,"
which includes Booker T. Washington in a list of seven names and, later in
the poem, praises him alongside W.E.B. Du Bois: "It's a long step to Booker
T. Washington / Building Tuskegee, / To Dr. W.E.B. Du Bois building a culture for America" (2: 269–77; lines 214–16). Finally, Booker T. Washington
is briefly mentioned in at least two later poems by Hughes that cover black
American history, "Prelude to Our Age" and "A Ballad of Negro History."

Because "Ballad of Booker T." is one of Hughes's most obviously complex poems, particularly when compared to the shorter and seemingly
simpler forms such as "Mother to Son" or "The Negro Speaks of Rivers,"
an extended analysis of the poem can potentially be sustained without
bringing in additional considerations or resources. Still, you may wish to
widen your understanding of Hughes's views on Washington by considering his other references to both the man and his far-reaching and lasting influence. Another approach would be to combine two or more of the
topics and strategies outlined below into a single essay, such as an essay
exploring the topic of revision as it relates to both the poem's changing
form through the various drafts and to the poet's changing views of the
poem's subject.

TOPICS AND STRATEGIES
Form and Genre

Sample Topics:

1. **Definitions of ballad:** Explore various definitions of the term
   ballad, and determine which particular definitions best describe
   Hughes's poem "Ballad of Booker T."

In addition to the poem "Ballad of Booker T.," Hughes wrote
no fewer than twenty-four poems that bear a title beginning

with "Ballad of. . . ." You may be interested in researching the term and in exploring some or all of Hughes's so-called ballads. Pay particular attention to the apparent purpose of Hughes's ballads, the presence or absence of dialogue, the presence or absence of any challenges to authority, the line length and meter, and anything else that might relate to the specific definitions of the ballad that you have located and incorporated into your essay.

2. **Philosophies of composition:** Analyze Hughes's composition of the poem "Ballad of Booker T." by reviewing various drafts of the poem that are available on the Internet.

Locate and analyze the four drafts and final version of the poem by Hughes that are available online at two locations hosted by the Library of Congress; see the entries for "African American Odyssey" and "Words and Deeds in American History" in the Bibliography and Online Resources section at the end of this chapter. (As URLs change frequently, you may need to enter the poem's title into a search field at these Library of Congress websites to locate the drafts.) The drafts show the poem in various stages of composition; review them carefully to see what they can tell you about Hughes's experiences in writing and revising the poem and, more generally, about the revision process itself. Take note of the dates on the different drafts of the poem. These dates may illustrate a point that students may have heard before but all too rarely practice: Good writers give themselves at least a little bit of time between each stage of the revision process. Take note, too, of the messiness of the drafts of the poem. Revision can be a messy but important process in improving anyone's writing, even that of a gifted poet. Consider the changes in the form of the typed drafts of the poems as well as the significance of Hughes's handwritten notes on the various pages. For example, along the right-hand margin of the second draft of the poem, dated May 31, 1941, there is a column of three-letter combinations that seems to have something to do with the change in one line that reads in this draft "Said he, seek a star" but reads in the next draft, dated June 1,

1941, "And not afar." If analyzing the drafts and the final poem do not present you with enough material for your essay, you may consider including a discussion of how Hughes's writing process resembles or differs from Edgar Allan Poe's account of how he wrote "The Raven," as outlined in his widely anthologized essay "Philosophy of Composition." For more on revising poems in general and on Hughes's revision process in particular, see Phyllis Brooks Bartlett's study of Hughes's and several other authors' revision practices, *Poems in Process*.

Compare and Contrast Essays

Sample Topics:

1. **Reassessing Booker T. Washington:** Compare and contrast two or more poems by Hughes on Washington, including the poem "Ballad of Booker T." Washington also receives positive treatment in Hughes's first novel, *Not Without Laughter.*

   Hughes's reassessment of Washington may parallel his reassessment of Mahatma Gandhi, whom he criticized in a number of poems in the 1920s and 1930s (perhaps most famously in "Goodbye Christ" but also in "Merry Christmas," for example) only to praise him in several later poems, including "Gandhi Is Fasting" (3: 281–82). If space and time allow, you may choose to address Hughes's reassessments of both leaders and even go on to develop your essay further by exploring possible reasons for this sort of reassessment of racial, ethnic, and national leaders in Hughes's poetry and other writings.

2. **Booker T. in poetry:** Compare and contrast Hughes's treatment of Booker T. Washington in the poem "Ballad of Booker T." with Washington's portrayal in the writings of one or more other poets.

   Explore how one or more other poets treat Washington and compare and contrast their treatment with that of Hughes. You may want to begin thinking about this topic by comparing Hughes's "Ballad of Booker T." with a second ballad, "Booker T. and W.E.B.," which was written by the more contemporary black poet Dudley Randall. You may want to consider how small details in both poems help register and reveal each speaker's feelings about the man. A developed discussion may require that you become more familiar with Washington's (and perhaps W.E.B. Du Bois's) program of racial uplift.

Bibliography and Online Resources for "Ballad of Booker T."

"African American Odyssey." Library of Congress. http://www.loc.gov/exhibits/ odyssey/archive/07/0708/7-08001.html. Downloaded on February 25, 2009.

Brooks Bartlett, Phyllis. *Poems in Process.* New York: Oxford UP, 1951.

"Booker T. Washington Delivers the 1895 Atlanta Compromise Speech." History Matters: The U.S. Survey Course on the Web. American Social History Project / Center for Media and Learning (Graduate Center, CUNY) and Center for History and New Media (George Mason University). http://historymatters. gmu.edu/d/39/. 31 March 2006. Downloaded on February 25, 2009.

"Words and Deeds in American History." Library of Congress. http://lcweb2. loc.gov/ammem/mccquery.html. Downloaded on February 25, 2009.

Brundage, W. Fitzhugh. *Booker T. Washington and Black Progress: Up from Slavery 100 Years Later.* Gainesville: UP of Florida, 2003.

"THE NEGRO
ARTIST AND THE
RACIAL MOUNTAIN"

READING TO WRITE

L ANGSTON HUGHES's essay "The Negro Artist and the Racial Mountain" first appeared in *The Nation* on June 23, 1926, and has since
been reprinted numerous times. Although the essay was published early
in his career, it has often been read (perhaps rightly so) as the artistic
manifesto for Hughes's entire poetic career.

Hughes opens the essay by criticizing one black poet for, he writes,
"subconsciously" desiring to be white, and in the paragraphs that follow,
he illustrates what he means by giving examples of how many middle-
and upper-class African Americans in the early 20th century would seek
to imitate the values of the dominant white culture, such as reading
white publications and "go[ing] to white theaters and white movies" (32),
marrying light-skinned partners, and avoiding popular black music (particularly the spirituals, blues, and jazz). This same group, he charges later
in the essay, seeks to limit the artistic expressions of black artists: "the
better-class Negro" or "the more advanced among his own group"—as
Hughes calls this group with more than a hint of sarcasm—"would tell
the artist what to do" (33). By way of illustration, Hughes embeds what
may be a brief account of his own experiences of receiving praise from
well-heeled black readers only after his own first book, *The Weary Blues*,
had been "accepted by a prominent New York publisher" (34).

After criticizing the black middle and upper classes in the essay,
Hughes clearly places his hopes as an individual and a poet on the black

lower classes. He sees in them both a freedom from expectations as well as a source of artistic inspiration. These "low-down folks" (32), as Hughes calls them, are not concerned with appearing respectable to white readers and thus do not pressure the black writer to focus only on certain themes and avoid others. For the black artist who can resist the pressures to paint only pleasant pictures of likewise black individuals, Hughes also writes, the black lower classes present "a great field of unused material ready for his art" and "sufficient matter to furnish a black artist with a lifetime of creative work" (33). At least two main themes are central to this essay: the struggle of some blacks to gain respectability at the cost of losing their racial distinctiveness and the artistic fertility of the black lower classes. Of course, you will likely see a number of other themes and other concerns to write about in connection with Hughes's essay.

Any strong discussion of a literary work starts with a close, engaged reading of the text. Print out or photocopy the essay and underline or highlight important phrases, repeated words, and related images on your photocopy. Ask questions and make observations about themes and language, perhaps beginning with the opening claim that Hughes makes, that the statement "I want to be a poet—not a Negro poet" reflects a hidden desire to actually be white. How convincing is this opening argument? For example, you may consider if you know of past or present pressures on black people to adopt white standards. You may also note peculiarities in the language of the essay related to this point; for example, Hughes uses the term *subconsciously* here and later uses the word *unconsciously* when making a similar point about the hidden desire to be white (32, 33). You may even develop an opinion about Hughes's casual use of Freudian psychoanalysis, with its claims about our unconscious motivations and about the ability of the psychoanalyst to move past surface meaning (that is, what we think we are saying) in order to discover in us the truer and deeper meaning, of which we are individually not aware (that is, what we are really saying). At this point, your ideas may be broad and undefined, but you will have generated your own material that can be used, in whole or in part, in a focused and developed paper on this essay.

In talking about the pressures on the black artist, for example, Hughes's essay also presents you with the opportunity to conduct outside research and explore some specific examples of the pressures that Hughes identifies. Ideally, your examples will have something to do with Hughes. For example, you may be interested in exploring W.E.B. Du Bois's limiting ideas on what makes good racial art (see, for example, Du Bois's essay "Criteria of Negro Art" and the questions that he poses in the symposium in *The Crisis* titled "How Shall The Negro Be Portrayed?"). A second possible topic would be the influence of the patronage of a wealthy white woman, Charlotte Mason, on Hughes's works and career. Review the different topics and strategies for further ideas of how you might develop your essay more fully.

TOPICS AND STRATEGIES
Language, Symbols, and Imagery
Sample Topics:

1. **American music and African-American music:** Establish and explore the connections between Hughes's essay "The Negro Artist and the Racial Mountain" and the poem "When Malindy Sings" by Paul Laurence Dunbar, a famous and accomplished poet writing and publishing a number of decades before Hughes's essay appeared in print.

   In "The Negro Artist and the Racial Mountain," Hughes praises African-American musical innovations—including the spirituals, the blues, and jazz—at the expense of what he calls "drab melodies in white folks' hymnbooks" (33). Read Paul Laurence Dunbar's playful and well-crafted poem "When Malindy Sings," and analyze how Dunbar's poem, published in 1895, embodies some or all of the values that Hughes embraces decades later in his essay. Your essay may be enriched by discussing the extent of Dunbar's influence on Hughes.

2. **Hughes as prophet:** Hughes styles himself as a prophet of his people in more ways than one. Write an essay that identifies and comments on the direct and indirect references to being a prophet in the essay "The Negro Artist and the Racial Mountain." Consider developing the essay further by locating some sort of prophecy (in a metaphoric sense of the word) in one or more of his poems.

In "The Negro Artist and the Racial Mountain," the young Hughes writes about the black artist needing "to climb [the mountain] in order to discover himself and his people" (32), using here a metaphor that suggests the story of Moses. Later he writes in the essay that the black artist, until recently, has been "a prophet with little honor" (34). Much later in his poetic career, as discussed in the second volume of the Rampersad biography, Hughes continued to view himself in this role of prophet-poet (see Rampersad, *The Life of Langston Hughes,* 2:85). In this essay, you may present these examples of Hughes as prophet and perhaps even find that one or more of his poems anticipate specific and dramatic social changes of the latter half of the 20th century. You may choose, for example, to focus on how his poetry anticipates one or more aspects of the civil rights era (such as the gradual desegregation of schools and lunch counters across the country) or demonstrate how Hughes gives early and clear expression to the later slogan "black is beautiful." Your essay will benefit from some general research on and discussion of the topic or topics that you have identified both in Hughes's poems and in a later period in African-American history. If you choose to focus on the slogan "black is beautiful," for example, you may wish to read some or all of *The Autobiography of Malcolm X,* paying particular attention to the author's discussions of the interconnectedness of skin color, hairstyles, language, and racial pride. You may want to define the term *prophet* in your essay, emphasizing its metaphorical applications: The prophet is often an individual, for example, who is intimately connected to the masses but does not belong among them.

Compare and Contrast Essays

Sample Topics:

1. **Hughes's essay as manifesto for his poetry:** Explore one or more ways in which the ideals that are stated in Hughes's essay "The Negro Artist and the Racial Mountain" are manifested in his poetry.

In exploring the topic of reading Hughes's essay "The Negro Artist and the Racial Mountain" as a manifesto for his poetry, you may want initially to consider focusing on poems written around the same time as the essay, such as those collected in his first two volumes, *The Weary Blues* (1926) and *Fine Clothes to the Jew* (1927). You may also expand the topic to include a discussion not just of the influence of blues but also the later influences of boogie-woogie and bebop, two later forms of black popular music, on his poetry. Hughes writes in the prefatory note to the volume of poetry *Montage of a Dream Deferred* (1951), which shows this new influence, that like bebop, his "poem on contemporary Harlem . . . is marked by conflicting changes, sudden nuances, sharp and impudent interjections, broken rhythms, and passages sometimes in the manner of the jam session, sometimes the popular song, punctuated by the riffs, runs, breaks, and disc-tortions of the music of a community in transition" (Hughes, *The Collected Works of Langston Hughes* 3:21). With more extensive reading of his poetry, you may also find your own, perhaps more surprising, connections between Hughes's essay and his poetry. In the poem "Crossing," for example, the speaker talks about going "up on the mountain" all by himself and being exposed to "a high cold wind" and "an icy stream." You may want to read this poem as a poetic reworking of Hughes's essay and perhaps even as a personal reflection by Hughes on the cold reception that he was given by many middle- and upper-class African Americans because of his focus on popular art forms, particularly the blues. Carefully reading the published reviews of his works when they first came out, if you can locate these materials, is an excellent and interesting way to understand how Hughes's contemporaries reacted to his poetry. For a collection of these reviews, see Tish Dace's *Langston Hughes: The Contemporary Reviews.*

2. **Poetry of Langston Hughes and Countee Cullen:** Compare and contrast the form and content of the poet's works with those of Countee Cullen. You may also wish to address more directly the two poets' ideas about aesthetics and the proper subjects for black poetry.

It is commonplace among critics to identify Cullen as the poet who is named and criticized by Hughes in the opening sentences of his essay "The Negro Artist and the Racial Mountain." Hughes criticizes this poet for "be[ing] afraid of being himself" and for rejecting the race-specific label of "Negro poet." Review at least three of Cullen's poems as well as his sonnet "Yet Do I Marvel" and consider the question of whether Cullen is any less a "Negro poet" than Hughes. Your answer may depend entirely on how you define "Negro poet"; a section of the opening of your essay may be dedicated to defining this term in more than one way, perhaps including but certainly moving past the obvious definition of a "Negro poet" as simply an African-American individual who writes poetry. To further develop your essay and to learn more about the other poet being considered here, you may want to read Cullen's review of Hughes's first volume of poetry, which includes the following statement:

> Taken as a group the selections in this book seem one-sided to me. They tend to hurl this poet into the gaping pit that lies before all Negro artists in the confines of which they become racial artists instead of artists pure and simple. There is too much emphasis here on strictly Negro themes, and this is probably an added reason for my coldness toward the jazz poems—they seem to set a too definite limit upon an already limited field (qtd. in "Langston Hughes Revisited and Revised." Tidwell and Ragar 5).

You may wish to consider if Hughes's "racial mountain" is the same thing as Cullen's "gaping pit." Are these simply two different perspectives on the same challenge facing the black poet in the early decades of the 20th century?

3. **Changing duties of the artist:** Compare and contrast the early essay "The Negro Artist and the Racial Mountain" with Hughes's later essay "To Negro Writers" (1935) in order to determine if the differences in the two essays illustrate a change in Hughes's outlook on the role of literature in shaping race relations and social life in the United States.

You may note, for example, that "The Negro and the Racial Mountain" focuses on the need for the individual artist to have integrity and to create what she feels she must create, whereas "To Negro Writers" disparages poets who want to write about the moon, for example, and includes a quick, biting reference to an actual lynching in order to show how conventional poetic subjects can be irrelevant in a time of crisis. The moon, he writes, "[s]hines over Cordie Cheek's grave, down South" (133). However, you may note that Hughes's first volume of poetry features at least three poems in which the moon figures prominently, and the uncollected poems published before 1930 include at least five more (Hughes, *The Collected Works of Langston Hughes* 1: 153–54, 169, 183, 192–93), as does his later volume *Fields of Wonder* (1947). You may not simply want to show that Hughes is inconsistent or contradicts himself; rather, you may wish to show that Hughes is a complex and evolving artist and person, perhaps even showing that his works from different decades reflect some of the key concerns of those particular years. Relevant sections on Hughes's aesthetics and politics in the biographies of Hughes may prove helpful as you develop your ideas for the essay.

4. **Langston Hughes versus George S. Schuyler:** Contrast the views of Hughes and Schuyler on the topic of African-American art, as expressed in their respective essays "The Negro Artist and the Racial Mountain" and "The Negro-Art Hokum."

Hughes's essay "The Negro Artist and the Racial Mountain" was published as a rebuttal to Schuyler's essay "The Negro-Art Hokum," which appeared in the previous issue of *The Nation* (June 16, 1926) and which sharply challenged the idea that black Americans were producing culturally distinctive art. Schuyler famously asserts, for example, that "the Aframerican is merely a lampblackened Anglo-Saxon" (97), someone who works alongside and who speaks like, dresses like, and worships like the European Americans surrounding him. In the end, you may wish to argue that one side is more compelling than the other, or you may wish to argue that both sides have merit and that the truth lies somewhere between the two. In any case, you will want to present a clear and reasoned argument in your paper.

Bibliography for "The Negro Artist and the Racial Mountain"

Cullen, Countee. "Poet on Poet." *Opportunity* 4 (4 March 1926): 73–74.

Dace, Tish. *Langston Hughes: The Contemporary Reviews.* New York: Cambridge UP, 1997.

Du Bois, W.E.B. "The Criteria of Negro Art." *The Crisis,* Vol. 32, No. 6, October 1926: 290–97.

Hughes, Langston. "To Negro Writers." 1935. *The Collected Works of Langston Hughes.* Columbia: U of Missouri P, 2002. 131–33.

———. "The Negro Artist and the Racial Mountain." 1926. *The Collected Works of Langston Hughes.* Columbia: U of Missouri P, 2002. 31–36.

Kelley, James. "The Crisis: The Negro in Art—How Shall He Be Portrayed? A Symposium." *Encyclopedia of the Harlem Renaissance.* Vol. 1. Ed. Cary D. Wintz and Paul Finkelman. New York: Routledge, 2004. 267–68.

Malcolm X. *The Autobiography of Malcolm X.* New York: Ballantine, 1992.

Rampersad, Arnold. *The Life of Langston Hughes, Volume II: I Dream a World.* New York: Oxford UP, 1988.

Rampersad, Arnold, ed. and intro. *The Collected Works of Langston Hughes.* Vol. 1. *The Poems: 1921–1940.* Columbia: U of Missouri P, 2001. 16 vols.

Schuyler, George S. "The Negro-Art Hokum." *The Portable Harlem Renaissance Reader.* Ed. David Levering Lewis. New York: Penguin, 1995. 96–99.

Tidwell, John Edgar, and Cheryl R. Ragar. "Langston Hughes Revisited and Revised." *Montage of a Dream: The Art and Life of Langston Hughes.* Ed. John Edgar Tidwell, Arnold Rampersad, and Cheryl R. Ragar. Columbia: U of Missouri P, 2007. 2–18.

Tracy, Steven C. "To the Tune of Those Weary Blues." New York: Amistad, 1993.

THE BIG SEA

READING TO WRITE

I T IS easy to read Hughes's 1940 autobiography, *The Big Sea*, as a factual record of his life, but as is no doubt true of all autobiographies, this work "omits some revealing matters of substance, twists some, and imagines others" (Berry 53). Faith Berry's biography of Hughes shows that even though "[n]ot everything adds up exactly as he presented it" (105), Hughes's firsthand account of the first half of his life is still useful in developing a fuller understanding of the development of the man in general and the evolution of Hughes as an artist in particular. Hughes's occasional departure from the factual record, however, invites us to read this first volume of his autobiography much in the way that we might read one of his novels, looking, for example, at the presentation of one or more themes or at the development of one or more specific characters.

As with any literary work, Hughes's autobiography can be read for what is omitted just as much as for what is included. For example, Hughes's two main biographers, Berry and Rampersad, have observed that *The Big Sea* contains little to no information on Hughes's radical views and publications from the 1930s. The volume ends just before it would have had to address, chronologically, Hughes's most overtly leftist, political, radical period. This omission can be attributed at least in part to "the backlash against radicalism as a result of the Nazi-Soviet Pact of 1939" (McLaren 1). Nonetheless, *The Big Sea* presents a number of comments that might hint at Hughes's more radical views, even if they are not treated directly. For example, in the first section of the autobiography, Hughes makes positive statements in regard to at least two early 20th-century radical groups, the Bolshevik revolutionaries in Russia and the Mexican revolutionists Pancho Villa and Emiliano Zapata. Similarly, in numerous places in the second section, he makes direct and critical observations about how "[t]he white man dominates Africa" and takes Africa's resources at will, including its young men to serve in "Europe's colonial armies" (95). The section on Africa also shows how American sailors exploit the African population in several ways.

The Big Sea is divided into three sections of almost equal length, arranged in roughly chronological order. The first section, "Twenty One," gives information about his early years, with particular focus on his conflicted relationship with his parents, and ends with Hughes turning 21 and attempting to make a clean break with the past by sailing for Africa. The second section, "The Big Sea," takes its name from Hughes's experiences working on various freight boats crossing the Atlantic Ocean. The section describes in short, vivid sections his experiences sailing along the west coast of Africa, as well as his experiences in Rotterdam, Paris, Genoa, and other European cities. The third and final section, "Black Renaissance," takes up a topic mentioned briefly a number of times in the first two sections—the vibrant black cultural scene of Harlem. Here, Hughes presents the first written, firsthand account of the Harlem Renaissance by a full participant. As suggested in a 1940 letter from Hughes to Arna Bontemps, this section was "supposedly cut in its final draft stages because 'it was [the] part publishers liked least and thought had the least of me in it" (McLaren 11). Cary D. Wintz's book *The Harlem Renaissance, 1920–1940* contains a copy of an original one-page "readers' report" (348) that also reflects the general criticisms of the submitted manuscript and that suggests at least some cuts were made before the autobiography was published.

The autobiography presents a number of themes that also appear in Hughes's other writings. Steven Carl Tracy, for example, reads the "Salvation" section in *The Big Sea* as evidence of Hughes's skepticism toward religion even while the author writes of many aspects of black daily life, including Christian worship services and songs: "Clearly Hughes did not exalt spirituals and gospel music because of any fervent belief in Christianity. The 'Salvation' chapter in *The Big Sea* outlines his traumatic (non-) conversion experience that left him doubting the existence of a Jesus who had not come to rescue him" (*Historical Guide to Langston Hughes,* 103). Other recurring subjects include the tragic mulatto theme and the interest in race relations in the United States and abroad. As reflected in his autobiographical account, Hughes is particularly attentive to race relations in the countries that he visits, including West African nations as well as Mexico and France. In Paris, for example, Hughes writes that he had no difficulties sharing a boardinghouse room and bed with a white woman, but he also witnessed hostility toward foreign laborers and learns from other black Americans in the city that his career opportunities are limited: "There're plenty of French people for ordinary work. 'Less you can play jazz or tap dance, you'd just as well go back home" (125). Perhaps because of Hughes's extensive travels and his strong interest in race relations around the world, his autobiography had wide-reaching influence. Amiri Baraka's foreword to the 1986 edition of *The Big Sea* attests to Hughes's worldwide impact. Hughes "catalyzed black literary development internationally" (qtd. in Steven Carl Tracy, *Historical Guide to Langston Hughes*, 203).

Hughes's autobiography is of value to students of the author, because it deals with the development of Hughes as a poet. *The Big Sea* mentions several works, including the poems "The Negro Speaks of Rivers" and "The Weary Blues" as well as the short story "African Morning." Often when Hughes mentions a specific title in *The Big Sea*, he also makes brief but interesting observations about his own creative processes. In describing some of his earliest poems written as a graduating senior in high school, for example, he makes a distinction between two types of writing: "I had a whole notebook full of poems by now, and another one full of verses and jingles. I always tried to keep verses and poems apart, although I saw no harm in writing verses if you felt like it, and poetry if you could" (64). Just two pages later, in his brief discussion of "The Negro Speaks of Rivers," he writes that generally all he has to do is get started on the poem: "there are seldom many changes in my poems, once they're written down . . . the rest of the poem . . . flows from those first few lines, usually right away" (66). This method of composition probably worked well for Hughes when writing poems in free verse or in the form of blues lyrics, but when writing poems with a more formal structure (with fixed meter and rhyme), such as "The Weary Blues" or "Ballad of Booker T.," he revises his work more extensively. On the topic of creating the poem "The Weary Blues," for example, Hughes writes in *The Big Sea*: "I worked and worked on it—something that seldom happens to any of my poems" (90).

Although the autobiography has several recurring themes and central concerns, the narrative is fragmented and covers a lot of material. This combined lack of structural unity and wide range of subject matter may initially make the writer's task more difficult. One viable approach would be to approach *The Big Sea* as if it were a novel and, just as you would when writing an essay on a novel, settle on a clear topic and limit your discussion to items that are closely related to it. Review the different topics and strategies in the following section for ideas on how you might develop and focus your analysis of the work. Having chosen a topic or set of related topics for your essay, you may want to read the relevant sections of *The Big Sea* a second time in order to identify important passages and developments that will fit meaningfully into your discussion and analysis.

TOPICS AND STRATEGIES
Themes
Sample Topics:

1. **Racial identity and passing:** Explore Hughes's treatment in *The Big Sea* of the moments in his life that led him to question or to assert his own racial identity.

   A good deal of *The Big Sea* addresses the question of Hughes's racial identity. He may be taken for either black or Mexican in Mexico and even in the United States, for example, but is not dark enough to pass for black among native Africans. You may wish to focus on one or more specific instances in the autobiography, such as the two short scenes in which Hughes has the opportunity to pass for Mexican or admit to being a black American; see the short chapter "Back Home" in the first section of *The Big Sea*. Two other chapters to consider for discussion in an essay on this topic may be "Africa" and "Burutu Moon" in the second section of the autobiography.

2. **Color lines and racial prejudices:** Explore how Hughes uses the accounts of his many travels in *The Big Sea* to reflect on race relations and racial and ethnic prejudices in the United States and abroad.

   In his autobiography *The Big Sea*, Hughes addresses the different opportunities afforded to (or denied) American whites and blacks, light- and dark-skinned Mexicans, and American Indians based on their race, ethnicity, and skin color. You may wish to begin your treatment of this subject by exploring his father's reported experiences in the United States and Mexico as well as his father's reported treatment of the different people with whom he had dealings. You may want to focus on the chapters "Negro," "Father," and "Mexico Again" in the first section of *The Big Sea*. For a longer essay, you may wish to develop this topic further by exploring how Hughes uses a variety of terms—*Negro, colored, brownskin,* and others—throughout his autobiography when referring to black Americans. You may find, for example, that he does not use these terms consistently or equally and that he seems to prefer one or two terms when writing about himself and uses a wider range of terms more frequently when writing about other people.

3. **Ceaseless movement and freedom from prejudices:** Explore how Hughes's autobiography *The Big Sea* presents what Richard Wright has called the "jerky transitions" and "ceaseless movement" of his life and explore what connections may exist between the movement in Hughes's life and his freedom from many common social prejudices.

In his 1940 review of *The Big Sea* in *The New Republic*, Richard Wright calls attention to the "jerky transitions" of Hughes's life and asserts that "this ceaseless movement" helped Hughes become the important literary figure that he is because it prevented him from "remaining in one place long enough to become a slave of prevailing Negro middle-class prejudices" (Wright 214). You may want to present and analyze two or more instances in *The Big Sea* in which Hughes seems to challenge common social prejudices.

4. **Lifelong suspicion of religion:** Harold Bloom identifies the "Salvation" chapter in Hughes's autobiography *The Big Sea* as one of many indications of the author's "lifelong suspicion of religion" (53). Explain this topic in terms of one or more of his writings.

Read and analyze the chapter "Salvation" and review the full text of *The Big Sea* in order to identify additional instances of this "lifelong suspicion." Consider developing your essay more fully by exploring how this same suspicion is manifested in other writings by Hughes, including his poem "Goodbye Christ," his essay "To Negro Writers," and his novel *Tambourines to Glory.* In order to develop a strong argument of your own, consider exploring the possibility that Hughes's position toward religion does not remain constant throughout his life.

5. **Illness and creativity:** Review Hughes's accounts of his illnesses in *The Big Sea* and determine whether or not you agree with Arnold Rampersad's conclusion that there is a strong and perhaps surprising connection between the poet's poor health and his creative output.

In his essay "The Origins of Poetry in Langston Hughes" and later in his influential autobiography, Arnold Rampersad argues that physical illness and general unhappiness are the sources of Hughes's best poetry. Examine Rampersad's argument and evidence. You may develop your paper more fully by working to develop other possible sources for Hughes's creative energies or to explore more generally how illness and creativity might indeed be strongly connected.

Character

Sample Topics:

1. **Characterization of Hughes's father:** Explore how Hughes presents his father in his autobiographical work *The Big Sea.*

In addition to a number of explicit comments about his father, Hughes makes a number of implicit statements through detailed characterization. Analyze the characterization of Hughes's father just as you might analyze the presentation and development (or lack of development) of a character in a more purely fictional work. You may wish to ask yourself if you agree that Hughes presents his father, in Arnold Rampersad's words, "as almost satanic, a figure who tempts his son with wealth if he would betray blacks and poetry" (*Big Sea* 35).

2. **Characterization of specific luminaries of the Harlem Renaissance:** Explore how Hughes uses his autobiography *The*

Big Sea as an opportunity to defend specific individuals and perhaps even to mock or attack others.

You may be interested in exploring how Hughes uses *The Big Sea* to praise his former patron, Charlotte Mason, even though their relationship had already ended. If the relationship between Hughes and Mason interests you, you may want to review the readers' report included in Cary D. Wintz's book, which voices the criticism that Hughes's manuscript says far too much in general about the patron, strays from the focus on Hughes, and gives advice that Hughes apparently did not follow. The relevant section of the readers' report reads: "Here the familiar criterion should be used: whatever deals with the relationship between her and him should be retained, but whatever deals with her other affairs, her charities, her philosophies, her contacts, should be boiled down to a sentence or two" (348). Other specific individuals of the Harlem Renaissance who may be defended, mocked, or attacked in *The Big Sea* are Carl Van Vechten, George Wilson Becton, Alain Locke, and Zora Neale Hurston.

History and Context

Sample Topics:

1. **Black experiences in post–World War I Europe:** Like many other black artists of the Harlem Renaissance, Hughes spent a substantial amount of time living in Paris and other cities of post–World War I Europe. Explore how the autobiography *The Big Sea* and perhaps other sources, by Hughes or other artists, set up parallels or contrasts between race relations in France (or, more generally, in Europe) and in the United States.

Other writings by Hughes that identify parallels or contrasts between race relations in France and in the United States include his short stories "Home," "Poor Little Black Fellow," and "The Blues I'm Playing." Substantial sections of Nella Larsen's novel *Quicksand* similarly explore the status of a black American in Denmark. After analyzing each text that you have selected, you may find that these and other sources demonstrate that France (and perhaps Europe in general) in the first few decades of the 20th century did not have strictly enforced segregation yet did not offer completely racially unbiased living opportunities for black Americans, either.

2. **The Harlem Renaissance:** Hughes's autobiography *The Big Sea* is often called the first written account of the Harlem Renaissance by someone who was a full participant. Use his statements in *The Big Sea* to reconstruct his attitude toward and view of the Harlem Renaissance.

Read the final sections of Hughes's autobiography *The Big Sea* to determine Hughes's position toward the Harlem Renaissance, a period or movement that had ended by the time he wrote and published his autobiography. Determine what he finds worthy of praise about the Harlem Renaissance and what he finds necessary to critique. Identify and discuss any instances of ironic distance or commentary on Hughes's part in his account of the Harlem Renaissance.

Bibliography for *The Big Sea*

Bloom, Harold, ed. *Langston Hughes*. Broomall, Penn.: Chelsea House, 1999.

Hughes, Langston. *The Big Sea*. 1940. *The Collected Works of Langston Hughes*. Ed. Joseph McLaren. Volume 13. Columbia: U of Missouri P, 2002. 16 vols.

McLaren, Joseph. "Introduction." *The Big Sea*. 1940. *The Collected Works of Langston Hughes*. Volume 13. Columbia: U of Missouri P, 2002. 1–16.

Rampersad, Arnold. "The Origins of Poetry in Langston Hughes." *The Southern Review* 21:3 (1985): 694–705.

———. "The Big Sea." *The Concise Oxford Companion to African American Literature*. Eds. William L. Andrews, Frances Smith Foster, and Trudier Harris. New York: Oxford UP, 2003.

Wintz, Cary D. *The Harlem Renaissance, 1920–1940*. New York: Taylor and Francis, 1996.

Wright, Richard. "Forerunner and Ambassador." Review of *The Big Sea*. In Michel Fabre. *Richard Wright: Books and Writers*. Jackson: UP of Mississippi, 1990, p. 214.

"THE BLUES I'M PLAYING"

READING TO WRITE

"THE BLUES I'm Playing," which was included in Hughes's 1934 collection of short stories, *The Ways of White Folk*, charts the course of a relationship that develops between a white patron and a black artist during the Great Depression. While the story can be read and appreciated on its own, it takes on greater significance when read in comparison to Hughes's biography, for the story retells—and even substantially revises—Hughes's own relationship with a wealthy white patron, Charlotte Mason, that began promisingly in 1927 and ended painfully in 1930.

As when reading most fiction, you may want to consider the role of the narrator in this particular story and whether or not the narrator seems neutral or biased. While the narrator may seem neutral at first, the details that the narrator provides subtly guide the reader to sympathize with the black artist and to praise her actions just as it steers the reader to feel cynicism, if not something much worse, toward the white patron and to question her motivations. As an active reader, you will want to be alert to how the very story that you are reading seeks to shape your views of specific characters in the story.

You may note, for example, how the story emphasizes the patron's desire to remove the artist from the very milieu that produced her and, parallel to this physical process of removal, the story reveals the patron's thinly veiled desire to gain greater control over the artist and her work. "I must get her out of Harlem," the patron says early in the story (76), and the narrator further reveals to the reader even more indicting thoughts of Mrs. Ellsworth: She "wishe[s] she could lift Oceola up bodily and take her away from all that, for art's sake" (78). The patron literally insists on taking Oceola up and away—first causing the musician to leave her home in Harlem for an apartment in the Village and to spend weekends in a mountain lodge in upstate New York and then causing her to leave New York altogether for Paris. Even in Paris, however, Oceola is able to locate and forge ties to a black community that appreciates her blues music.

You may note how the story presents the different reactions of the two women. Oceola remains mildly suspicious of her patron's motives and devoted to staying true to her own goals in life, whereas Mrs. Ellsworth is shown to be fascinated and controlling at the same time. The narrator seems to avoid answering questions that might cause the reader to reevaluate her or his view of Oceola. For example, the reader may wonder why Oceola so readily follows many of her patron's wishes that go against her own wishes, such as giving up the music teaching that she enjoyed so much. By contrast, the reader receives more than enough information on Mrs. Ellsworth's motives. The patron's fascination, the story hints, may be fueled in part by her erotic attraction to the other woman; as they share a bed at one point in the story, the patron remains "aware all the time of the electric strength of that brown-black body beside her" (78). By the story's end, the alert reader has easily received enough information about the patron to see her as blind to her own failings.

You may also note how the story sets up a subtle and sustained contrast between the two women. The narrator repeatedly reminds the reader, for example, that one is white, middle-aged, and widowed and the other is black, younger, and unmarried but involved in a long-term relationship with a man. Further, the narrator tells the reader at least twice that the white woman "sublimates" her experiences—that is, she seeks to transform certain sensations, such as sexual desire, into lofty thoughts and ideals—whereas the black woman lives life directly and embraces the sensations that life offers. The patron even thinks that books are a valid substitute for real experience, for example; she seeks to learn about Harlem by reading the novel *Nigger Heaven,* for example, and thinks that she understands the living conditions of the working poor because, "[a]fter all, she had read Thomas Burke on Limehouse" (77). In contrast, the character of Oceola Jones remains sympathetic because she does not abandon her values as an artist, insists on pursuing her own course in life (including marrying her longtime lover despite her patron's objections), and even confronts her patron at the story's end, drowning out the patron's chastising words with her own loud, black music. For an example of how the story's structure may influence the sympathies of critics and not just those of general readers, see the essay by Sandra Y. Govan listed at the end of this section. Govan walks the reader through the story in a thorough manner but seems to take the story's content largely at face value and does not ask, for example, how and why Oceola Jones comes across as such a likeable character.

If "The Blues I'm Playing" is a reworking of Hughes's firsthand experiences with white patronage, the reader may not be surprised to see the black artist presented as a more likeable character than the white patron. In order to fully explore the similarities and differences between the story and Hughes's own experiences with his patron Charlotte Mason, you may want to review volume one of Arnold Rampersad's biographical study and perhaps also *The Big Sea*, the first volume of Hughes's autobiography. (To locate the relevant information more efficiently in Rampersad's lengthy biography, use the table of contents and index of the biographies you consult.) In comparing the details of the story and of Hughes's experiences with Mason, you are likely to see a number of significant similarities and differences. For example, the artist character in the story seems different from Hughes, in terms of how he behaved toward his patron. Arnold Rampersad, for example, calls Hughes's behavior a "pathetic enslavement by Mrs. Mason" (200). Similarly, Hughes's own account in *The Big Sea* is about as different as it could be from the defiant, joyful protest against the controlling patron in the short story. Hughes writes:

> I cannot write here about that last half hour in the big bright drawing-room high above Park Avenue one morning, because when I think about it, even now, something happens in the pit of my stomach that makes me ill. That beautiful room, that had been so full of light and help and understanding for me, suddenly became like a trap closing in, faster and faster, the room darker and darker, until the light went out with a sudden crash in the dark. . . . (325)

You may want to compare this account by Hughes of the final scene with his patron to the final scene in "The Blues I'm Playing," noting the marked variances. In the final scene of the story, the black artist Oceola strongly expresses her own views, and rather than sensing that the room is shrinking and darkening, she fills it with her bold and energetic music, shaking the flowers in their vases and temporarily drowning out the patron's voice.

This brief discussion does not exhaust the topic of the similarities and differences between "The Blues I'm Playing" and Hughes's own experiences with a wealthy patron, nor is it meant as the only way to approach the short story. As the following suggested topics indicate, there are multiple approaches to the short story "The Blues I'm Playing."

TOPICS AND STRATEGIES
Themes
Sample Topics:

1. **The ways of white folks:** Explore how the short story "The Blues I'm Playing" develops the theme of white people's treatment (or mistreatment) of black people.

   The short story "Berry" is not one of the best works included in the volume *The Ways of White Folks,* but the story is significant because the volume's title appears in a passage from the story that encapsulates the theme of the volume as a whole. The title character in "Berry" says at one point: "[T]he ways of white folks, I mean some white folks, is too much for me. I reckon they must be a few good ones, but most of 'em ain't good—leastwise they don't treat me good. And Lawd knows, I ain't never done nothin' to 'em, nothin' a-tall" (114). Reread "The Blues I'm Playing," paying particular attention to the treatment or mistreatment of the main character, and explore whether or not Berry's observation applies equally to the main character, Oceola. Is she treated poorly or unfairly? If so, how?

2. **Influence of art on race relations:** Read Hughes's short story "The Blues I'm Playing" as a possible response to the belief embraced by W.E.B. Du Bois, Alain Locke, and other intellectual leaders of the Harlem Renaissance that good art by black artists will help secure racial equality for black Americans.

   At one point in the story, Oceola challenges the belief that good art by black artists will help secure racial equality for black Americans. In her mind, if not out loud, she voices her disagreement:

> And as for the cultured Negroes who were always saying that art would break down color lines, art could save the race and prevent lynchings! "Bunk!" said Oceola. "My ma and pa were both artists when it came to making music, and the white folks ran them out of town for being dressed up in Alabama. And look at the Jews! Every other artist in the world's a Jew, and still folks hate them." (79)

Explore the views of at least a couple of these "cultured Negroes"—focusing perhaps on essays by Du Bois ("Criteria of Negro Art") and Locke ("Enter the New Negro")—and contrast these views with Oceola's. Answering some or all of the following questions may help you develop the topic more fully: Do the essays by Du Bois and Locke seem to have more commonalities than differences? Do other works by Hughes seem to present views similar to Oceola's? Which view do you find the most convincing? You may find it worth noting that *The Ways of White Folks,* the collection of short stories in which "The Blues I'm Playing" appeared, was published in 1934. According to many critics, the Harlem Renaissance was rapidly fading if not already a thing of the past by 1934, yet segregation on the basis of race was still practiced and entrenched in many parts of the United States. Can this connection help further explain the skepticism in the story toward using art to improve race relations?

Character
Sample Topics:
1. **The female blues singer:** Explore how Oceola, the main character in the short story "The Blues I'm Playing," uses her art to assert her independence and possibly go on to connect this particular example to larger issues of black women blues singers (and, more generally, to black female artistry) in the early 20th century.

Since the early 1990s, a number of feminist scholars—including Hazel Carby and Cheryl Wall—have explored how women

blues singers used their music to voice their individual criticism of and resistance to social pressures in general and unful-
filling, constraining relationships in particular. Review some
of these studies (or parts, such as the section "Women, Migration and the Formation of a Blues Culture" in Carby's *Cultures
in Babylon*) and apply the insights that you have gained to your
analysis of the value of Oceola's art in Hughes's story. You may
also wish to include other treatments by Hughes of the female
blues singer, such as Harriet, one of the central characters in
his first novel, *Not Without Laughter.*

2. **Characterization through imagery:** Identify and discuss the
   images in the short story "The Blues I'm Playing" that are associated with and thereby help to characterize Mrs. Ellsworth. Do
   the same for Oceola. Reflect on how your close analysis of the
   imagery in the story contributes to your fuller understanding of
   the story as a whole.

In the course of searching for images that surround the two
main characters in "The Blues I'm Playing," you may come
to see an extreme imbalance: The narrator gives the reader
a wealth of imagery to associate with Mrs. Ellsworth (these
images deal mostly with her dress and with the furnishings
of her home, such as the vases full of flowers at the story's
end) but little imagery to associate with Oceola. If the reader
is indeed supplied with images to associate with Oceola (the
main image may perhaps be captured in the phrase from the
story "a rich velvet black . . . a hard young body . . ."), this second set of images seems to come to the reader through Mrs.
Ellsworth's perspective, not through the narrator's. Discuss
how these and other results of your analysis of the images contribute to your fuller understanding of the story as a whole.

Form and Genre

Sample Topics:

1. **Form and structure of the story:** Identify and discuss the formal techniques through which the short story "The Blues I'm
   Playing" is developed. In your discussion, consider the various

ways that you could analyze the form and structure of the story, including the story's use of narration, point of view, direct dialogue and summary dialogue, and conflict and resolution.

In *Langston Hughes: A Study of the Short Fiction,* Hans Ostrom writes that Hughes's stories are not experimentalist and are instead based on "simple narrative forms—the tale, the sketch, the parable, and deliberately undramatic reportage" (qtd. in *The Collected Works of Langston Hughes* 15:2). Explain whether or not you find that Ostrom's statement applies to the short story "The Blues I'm Playing." To develop your essay more fully, you may want to contrast the form of this story with that of a second short story, "Red-Headed Baby." In this second short story, for example, you may identify at least some experimentation in the way in which the story is developed, particularly in sentence structure and imagery.

2. **Black folk speech and art forms in the story:** Write an essay exploring the level of success that Hughes has in incorporating black folk speech and art forms in the short story "The Blues I'm Playing."

Hans Ostrom, in his *Langston Hughes: A Study of the Short Fiction,* suggests that Hughes is "interested in allowing colloquial language, the blues, gospel music, and the sound and sense of 'street speech' to inform the language of his short fiction" (qtd. in *The Collected Works of Langston Hughes* 15:2). Identify places in the story in which these elements surface. To widen your subject for a more developed essay, consider discussing Hughes's use of black vernacular and black art forms in one or more of his other works or consider comparing Hughes with one of his Harlem Renaissance contemporaries who also wrote prose fiction, such as Zora Neale Hurston or Jessie Fauset.

3. **Guy de Maupassant and Langston Hughes:** Explore the short stories of the French author Guy de Maupassant to determine to what extent he might have served as an influence on Hughes.

In *The Big Sea*, Hughes identifies the French writer Guy de Maupassant as an important influence on him: "I think it was de Maupassant who made me really want to be a writer and write stories about Negroes, so true that people in far-away lands would read them—even after I was dead" (51). The influence may show itself in any number of places, such as in the content of the stories, in the themes that are developed, or in the narrative techniques of the stories.

Compare and Contrast Essays

Sample Topics:

1. **Biographical parallels:** Drawing from one or more biographies of Hughes, identify and discuss the similarities and differences between the real experiences of Hughes with his patron Charlotte Mason and the fictional account of Oceola Jones's experiences with her patron, Dora Ellsworth, in the short story "The Blues I'm Playing." Construct an argument based on the most significant of these similarities and differences.

In discussing the parallels between the experiences of Hughes and Jones with their white patrons, you may want to address any or all of the following questions: How does the patron come to learn of the artist? How does the patron first react to the artist, and vice versa? What sorts of conversations and what level of intimacy do the patron and artist experience with each other? What expectations does the patron have of the artist? How is the artist's work positively and negatively affected by the patronage? How is racial difference a defining factor in the patron's view of the artist? In what ways do the home and dress of the patron in the story resemble the home and dress of the patron in Hughes's life? Does even the patron's talk about a person's "spirit" (81) echo the odd spiritualism of Hughes's patron, as presented in Rampersad's biography? How does the patronage end? Is there a final, dramatic scene of confrontation or simply a fading of contact? After addressing any or all of these questions and after identifying and answering a few questions of your own, you may wish to focus on how this short story may be rewriting as much as it is recording Hughes's own experiences with white patronage. You may wish to develop the essay further by considering what the story might say more generally about white patronage of black artists in the early 20th century or how the story also incorporates some of Zora Neale Hurston's life experiences along with those of Hughes into the character of Oceola Jones.

2. **Race relations in France and the United States:** Like Hughes and many other black artists of the Harlem Renaissance, the fictional character Oceola Jones in the short story "The Blues I'm Playing" lives in Paris for some time, practicing her art and interacting with white and black intellectuals and artists. Explore how this story and other sources, by Hughes or other artists, set up parallels or contrasts between race relations in France (or, more generally, in Europe) and in the United States.

Other writings by Hughes that set up parallels or contrasts between race relations in France and in the United States include his autobiographical work *The Big Sea* as well as his short stories "Home" and "Poor Little Black Fellow." Substantial sections of Nella Larsen's novel *Quicksand* similarly explore the status of a black American in Denmark. After analyzing each text that you have selected, you may find that these and other sources demonstrate that France (and perhaps Europe in general) in the first few decades of the 20th century did not have strictly enforced segregation yet did not offer completely racially unbiased living opportunities for black Americans, either.

3. **White patronage, condescension, segregation, and hypocrisy:** Compare and contrast Hughes's treatment of the white patronage of black artists in two or more of his short stories, including the short story "The Blues I'm Playing."

To develop a comparison and contrast essay that makes use of the short story "The Blues I'm Playing," you may wish to read one or more of Hughes's other short stories that focus extensively on the white patronage of black artists in the early 20th century, such as "Poor Little Black Fellow," "Slave on the Block," and "Rejuvenation Through Joy." You may wish to focus at least part of your analysis on the similar, angry confrontations at the end of many of these stories. A strong essay on this topic will go beyond the particulars of each story and make a larger argument about Hughes's views of the patronage system that was so important to Hughes and to many other artists of the Harlem Renaissance.

Bibliography for "The Blues I'm Playing"

Carby, Hazel. *Cultures in Babylon: Black Britain and African America.* London: Verso, 1999.

———. "It Jus Be's Dat Way Sometime: The Sexual Politics of Women's Blues." *Feminisms: An Anthology of Literary Theory and Criticism.* Ed. Robyn R. Warhol and Diane Price Herndl. Piscataway: Rutgers UP. 746–58.

Govan, Sandra Y. "The Paradox of Modernism in *The Ways of White Folks.*" *Montage of a Dream: The Art and Life of Langston Hughes.* Ed. John Edgar Tidwell, Arnold Rampersad, and Cheryl R. Ragar. Columbia: U of Missouri P, 2007. 147–65.

Hughes, Langston. *The Big Sea.* 1940. *The Collected Works of Langston Hughes.* Ed. Joseph McLaren. Vol. 13. Columbia: U of Missouri P, 2002.

Ostrom, Hans. *Langston Hughes: A Study of the Short Fiction.* New York: Twayne, 1993.

Story, Ralph D. "Patronage and the Harlem Renaissance: You Get What You Pay For." *College Language Association Journal* 32.3 (1989). 284–95.

Wall, Cheryl A. "Whose Sweet Angel Child? Blues Women, Langston Hughes, and Writing During the Harlem Renaissance." *GRAAT: Publication des Groupes de Recherches Anglo-Américaines de l'Université François Rabelais de Tours* 14 (1996): 63–72.

"FATHER AND SON"

READING TO WRITE

LANGSTON HUGHES's short story "Father and Son" was included in his 1934 collection of short stories, *The Ways of White Folks.* This is probably Hughes's longest short story, and it contains a wealth of material to present and discuss in an essay.

A careful reading of the story might begin with attempting to determine the story's setting. The narrator gives the place in the opening paragraphs: Big House Plantation somewhere in Georgia. Later in the story, the narrator reveals the somewhat more precise location of southern Georgia. However, the narrator does not name the year. You may want to make note of the small details in the story that may help you determine the era in which the story takes place. Some of these details suggest that the story takes place in the slavery era—Big House Plantation is a cotton plantation, for example, on which black workers unquestionably obey the white landowner and occupant of the Big House, with its "tall white pillars on the front porch" (128)—but other details work against this possibility, including at least three references to automobiles as well as references to a college for blacks somewhere far away and to plantation workers who are not slaves but rather "black servants and share croppers" (131). An essay analyzing "Father and Son" can spend some time exploring this question of setting and attempt to resolve or rectify these seemingly contradictory details in the story. If the story is not set in the slavery era but rather in some more recent period yet presents many details that seem to match an understanding of what slavery was like, you may be led to explore what the story is ultimately suggesting about the differences in life for black people on this Georgia plantation, both during and after the time of slavery.

"Father and Son" paints a portrait of a family of black sharecroppers and servants who are intimately but only unofficially related to the white male plantation owner. The Colonel, as he is called in the story, is married to a delicate white woman, and the couple have no children of their own. The Colonel takes his black housekeeper Cora as a lover and has, by her, a number of mixed-raced children. These children are treated better than the other workers on the plantation—they are the only ones on the plantation who are afforded a basic education, for example, and several are even sent away to black colleges—but he fails to fully acknowledge them as his own flesh and blood. The conflict emerges when, at the opening of the story, the reader learns that one of these mixed-race sons, Bert, is returning from college after a long absence for a visit to the Big House Plantation. Bert refuses to accept the second-class status assigned to him; he moves to shake his father's hand at one point in the story, for example, and enters the Big House through the front door, an act forbidden to him and all of his siblings. The conflict thus begins as a young man's defiance but quickly escalates to murder and a dual lynching.

The boldness of Bert's actions is made all the more clear by explicit and implicit contrasts in the story between Bert and his brother, Willie, who has never had difficulties obeying the restrictions imposed by the white father on his mixed-race children: "Willie and the Colonel got along fine, because Willie was docile and good-natured and nigger-like, bowing and scraping and treating white folks like they expected to be treated" (Hughes, *The Collected Works of Langston Hughes* 15: 138). In revising this story for inclusion in his 1963 collection of short stories, *Something in Common and Other Stories*, it is worth noting that Hughes made two changes in the description of Willie, deleting the term "old knotty-headed" and removing the word "nigger-like" (Hughes, *The Collected Works of Langston Hughes* 15: 138, 426n11–12). Thus, while you may certainly be able to write a successful essay that focuses exclusively on the final, collected version of the story, you may be interested in considering these revisions to "Father and Son" and perhaps revisions to other works by Hughes.

Another possibility for developing an essay on this short story would be to read one or more texts alongside "Father and Son" and to examine the similarities and differences between them. The wealthy white man as the father of a black male worker, along with the open secret of that relationship, is a common topic in African-American literature in the

19th century. You can find this subject treated in the opening section of Frederick Douglass's widely read *Narrative of the Life of Frederick Douglass*. This literary tradition is explored in a chapter in Leslie W. Lewis's 2007 study *Telling Narratives: Secrets in African American Literature*. Several other possible texts—including the ancient Greek myth of Oedipus and Victor Séjour's story of a slave's murder of his white master and father—are discussed as other possible parallel texts in one of the suggested sample topics. At least one critic has applied Freudian models, however lightly, to Hughes's writing; Anne P. Rice's *Witnessing Lynching: American Writers Respond* contains a short discussion of Hughes's poems "Justice" and "Christ in Alabama" as reflecting "the twisted oedipal relations between black males and a white patriarchy responsible for the mass rape of their mothers" (14).

To begin an essay on "Father and Son," start with a close reading of the story. Read for comprehension first. In your second and later readings, record your comments and reactions. Ask questions and make observations about themes and language, perhaps beginning with the opening description of the Big House Plantation. How important is the brief reference to the "tall white pillars on the front porch" (128), for example, and what roles do the front porch of the Big House play in later parts of the story? You may also note peculiarities in the language or the telling of the story that are related to the points that you are interested in exploring. For example, you may note that Hughes uses the term *white folks' nigger* no fewer than four times in the story, or you may note that the story contains glancing references to social revolutions of different kinds, including sudden mentions of Christ and Lenin (139), as well as a bizarre interruption of the story in the form of a vision (perhaps the narrator's or the author's) of the South being transformed through purging fire into something new:

> Bow down and pray in fear and trembling, go way back in the dark afraid; or work harder and harder; or stumble and learn; or raise up your fist and strike—but once the idea comes into your head you'll never be the same again. Oh, test tube of life! Crucible of the South, find the right powder and you'll never be the same again—the cotton will blaze and the cabins will burn and the chains will be broken and men, all of a sudden, will shake hands, black men and white men, like steel meeting steel. (139)

At this point, your ideas may be broad and undefined, but you will have generated your own material that can be used, in whole or in part, in a focused and developed paper on this story. The challenge often lies in selecting what exactly to focus on and in determining how exactly to make the pieces fit together.

Hughes's story also presents you with the opportunity to conduct outside research on related topics. For example, you may be interested in exploring the status of black sharecroppers in the post-slavery South or the literary tradition of the "tragic mulatto." Review the different topics and strategies in the following section for further ideas on how you might develop your paper idea more fully.

TOPICS AND STRATEGIES
Themes

Sample Topics:

1. **The ways of white folks:** Explore how the short story "Father and Son" develops the theme of white people's treatment (or mistreatment) of black people.

   The short story "Berry" may not be one of the better works included in the volume *The Ways of White Folks,* but the story is noteworthy for containing the volume's title in a passage that captures the theme of the entire volume. The title character in "Berry" says at one point: "[T]he ways of white folks, I mean some white folks, is too much for me. I reckon they must be a few good ones, but most of 'em ain't good—leastwise they don't treat me good. And Lawd knows, I ain't never done nothin' to 'em, nothin' a-tall" (114). Reread "Father and Son," paying particular attention to the behaviors of the main characters, and explore whether or not Berry's observation applies equally to Colonel Thomas Norwood, Bert, Cora, the white storekeeper, and other characters in "Father and Son."

2. **Fooling oneself and fooling others:** Discuss the places in the short story "Father and Son" in which the narrator points to the white father's own lack of awareness of his motivations

and his attempts to fool others by misrepresenting the way he actually feels.

Reread "Father and Son" carefully, and note the passages in the story that tell (through the narrative) or show (through the character's actions) how Colonel Thomas Norwood does not understand his own feelings even as he tries to mislead others in the story. You may be able to fuse these two topics into a single thesis, and write a unified essay around that thesis, if you reflect on how these two topics—not knowing one's true self and believing that one can mislead others—may be related. For example, you may find these topics related through the Colonel's unrealistic desire to have mastery over everything in his domain, including himself. You may also want to explore to what extent the Colonel seems successful or unsuccessful in fooling others into thinking that, for example, he is not excited to see Bert return from college for a visit home.

3. **Rebellion and independence:** Identify and discuss Bert's acts of rebellion, both large and small, in the short story "Father and Son."

   In the short story "Father and Son," Bert resolves "not to be a *white folks' nigger*" (139). Consider how you might define this term, which appears four times in the story and thus is worthy of critical attention. To develop your essay more fully, you may wish to contrast Bert's actions and thoughts with those of Willie. (This contrast of Bert and Willie will also give you the opportunity to make sense of why the two characters, despite their extreme differences in personality and their different behaviors in the story, share the same fate at the story's end.) You may also wish to explore the large and small acts of rebellion or assertions of independence by Bert's mother, Cora.

4. **Continuity and change:** Analyze the short story "Father and Son" in terms of the theme of how things change or do not change in the American South from the slavery era through Reconstruction into the modern age.

Details in the short story "Father and Son" show that while some things change, such as the presence of the "new-fangled autobuggy" in southern Georgia (132), other things do not. One passage from the short story, quoted more extensively in the opening section of this chapter, may be particularly worth focusing on: "Bow down and pray in fear and trembling, go way back in the dark afraid; or work harder and harder; or stumble and learn; or raise up your fist and strike—but once the idea comes into your head you'll never be the same again" (139). This passage may hint that there are choices as to what will become of the South in the modern age, with some of these choices ("pray in fear" and "go way back in the dark afraid") working against change and others working toward it. You may be interested in showing how the three options for change named in the passage—"or work harder and harder; or stumble and learn; or raise up your fist and strike"—may allude to the different ideas and goals of Booker T. Washington, W.E.B. Du Bois, and advocates of a socialist revolution. You may also be interested in determining—through a close reading of the story and perhaps other works by Hughes—what the author's preferences might be, what sort of change he might like to see and how he might like to see it come about.

Character

Sample Topics:

1. **Biracial characters:** Explore Hughes's presentation of challenges facing biracial characters in the short story "Father and Son" and at least one other work by Hughes.

For other treatments of biracial characters, you may want to look at the short stories "Red-Headed Baby" and "Mother and Child"; the play *Mulatto;* the embedded story in *The Big Sea* about the child of a white European man and black African woman; and the poems "Cross," "Mulatto," and "Christ in Alabama." At least two other poems—"Red Silk Stockings" and "Ruby Brown"—address the topic as well but focus on the black woman (rather than on the mixed-race child born to her) and on the economic pressures that might drive her to prostitution. You may want to read definitions and discussions of the literary tradition of the "tragic mulatta" or "tragic mulatto" and determine to what extent Hughes's story or other writings fall within or modify this tradition.

2. **The cruel parent:** Backing away from the dead body of her white lover, employer, and the father of her children, the character Cora whispers, "You's cruel, Tom" (149). Explore the character of the cruel parent in the short story "Father and Son."

You may wish to develop the essay more fully by discussing the actions of Cora, the black mother in the story, toward her son. What does she do that is kind or cruel? Is the range of the mother's possible actions more limited than that of the father? Another possibility for developing the essay more fully is to explore connections to one or more of Hughes's other stories or writings. For example, you may wish to analyze sections of *The Big Sea*, particularly those passages focusing on Hughes's father and mother, or discuss the short story "Poor Little Black Fellow," in which one character observes: "Most elderly people are terrible. . . . Especially parents" (102). Additional information on Hughes's relationship with his own father and mother can be found in the biographies by Berry and Rampersad.

History and Context

Sample Topics:

1. **Lynching:** Examine the treatment of lynching in the short story "Father and Son." Explore how the story does or does not accurately reflect the actual practice of lynching.

Review one or more reliable resources on actual lynchings, such as the photograph and postcard images at the "Without Sanctuary" Web site listed at the end of this chapter. Apply the information that you gain to Hughes's short story "Father and Son." You might ask, for example, if both the story and the studies or records of actual lynchings that you have reviewed say the same thing about the purposes of that practice. "Father and Son" presents lynching not simply as punishment for an individual who has flouted local customs but also as a message to others not to do the same. For example, an undertaker says to Bert's mother at one point in the story: "[D]on't you darkies go to bed until you see the bonfire. You all are gettin' beside yourselves around Polk County. We'll burn a few more of you if you don't watch out" (151). The story also closes with the comment that the "fun" of the lynching has been spoiled for the white mob because Bert is not caught alive and implies that a second, living black man must be lynched to appease the crowd (153). These details suggest that lynching was as much about entertainment and even bloodlust as it was about intimidation or some distorted sense of justice. You may want to reflect on what it means that a second black man—Willie, who by all accounts is "docile and good-natured and nigger-like" (138)—is also lynched at the story's end. Finally, you may be interested in exploring lynching as a subject in other short stories by Hughes, including "Home." As discussed in the chapter in this book on the poem "Song for a Dark Girl," Hughes also wrote a number of poems about lynching.

2. **Dating the story's setting through historical references:** Identify and explore some or all of the historical references in the short story "Father and Son." Use this information to improve your understanding of the story as a whole.

Among the topics that may be found and explained in the short story are the "new-fangled autobuggy" (132) and other references to automobiles, the "Spiritual Jubilee Singers" (135), the "Jim Crow [rail]car" (135, 137), "the Institute in Atlanta" (137), the references to black people moving north to escape the restrictive race laws of the South (135, 138), and "the Scottsboro trials and the Camp Hill shootings" (140). Decide which of the historical references that you have identified in the story and explored may fit into a focused essay. You may want to use some or all of these historical references, for example, to determine the time in which the story is set, and you may then want to explore how this knowledge of when the story takes place affects how one can read and understand the work. Or you may be interested in exploring how the short story attaches itself through these many references to the much larger and painful history of black and white race relations in the United States.

Form and Genre

Sample Topics:

1. **Retelling of Oedipus or other story:** Explore how the short story "Father and Son" might be seen as a retelling of the ancient Greek myth of Oedipus, who returns to his homeland after a long absence and kills his own father.

   Greek myth has often provided a structure for many later writers to follow, and you may want to read one or more versions of the Oedipus tales in order to develop a full comparison between the myth and Hughes's short story. For example, you may find that subtle details in Sophocles' drama of Oedipus—such as the main character thinking that he knows more than he really does—are reflected in Hughes's story. You may consider developing your essay in a related direction by exploring the meaningful connections or similarities between "Father and Son" and an earlier story by another author. For example, Hughes's story has much in common with "The Mulatto," Victor Séjour's short story written more than 50 years earlier.

2. **Form and structure of the story:** Identify and discuss the formal techniques through which the short story "Father and Son" is developed. In planning your essay, consider all of the ways in which you might talk about how the story is told, including that story's use of point of view, direct dialogue and summary dialogue, and conflict and resolution.

   In *Langston Hughes: A Study of the Short Fiction*, Hans Ostrom writes that Hughes's stories are not experimentalist and are instead based on "simple narrative forms—the tale, the sketch, the parable, and deliberately undramatic reportage" (qtd. in *The Collected Works of Langston Hughes* 15: 2). Explain whether or not you find that Ostrom's statement applies to "Father and Son." You may want to carefully reread sections V and VI, for example, and consider how the narrator's voice and shaping of the story may be more obvious in those sections than it is in the opening part of the story. To develop your essay more fully, you may want to compare the form of this story with that of a second short story, "Red-Headed Baby," which also addresses the theme of biracial children. In this second story, you may identify more experimentation in the way in which the story is developed, particularly in sentence structure and the use of imagery.

Bibliography and Online Resources for "Father and Son"

Berry. Faith. *Langston Hughes: Before and Beyond Harlem.* New York: Citadel, 1992.

Hughes, Langston. *The Big Sea.* 1940. *The Collected Works of Langston Hughes.* Ed. Joseph McLaren. Vol. 13. Columbia: U of Missouri P, 2002.

Lewis, Leslie W. *Telling Narratives: Secrets in African American Literature.* Urbana: U of Illinois P, 2007.

Ostrom, Hans. *Langston Hughes: A Study of the Short Fiction.* New York: Twayne, 1993.

Rampersad, Arnold. *The Life of Langston Hughes.* Vol. 1. *1902–1941: I, Too, Sing America.* New York: Oxford UP, 2002.

———. *The Life of Langston Hughes.* Vol. 2. *1941–1967: I Dream a World.* New York: Oxford UP, 2002.

Rice, Anne P. *Witnessing Lynching: American Writers Respond.* Piscataway, N.J.: Rutgers UP, 2003.

Séjour, Victor. "The Mulatto." Eds. Henry Louis Gates, Jr. and Nellie Y. McKay. *Norton Anthology of African American Literature.* New York: W.W. Norton, 1996.

"Without Sanctuary: Photographs and Postcards of Lynching in America." Collection of James Allen and John Littlefield. Available online. URL: http://www.withoutsanctuary.org/main.html. Downloaded on March 3, 2009.

"SLAVE ON THE BLOCK"

READING TO WRITE

Langston Hughes's short story "Slave on the Block" was included in his 1934 collection, *The Ways of White Folks,* and remains one of his mostly widely anthologized and widely taught short stories. "Slave on the Block" tells the story of an artistic white couple—Michael and Anne Carraway—who live in New York City's Greenwich Village in the early 1930s and who are enchanted with what they see as the primitivism of the black culture of Harlem. They take into their home a young black man, Luther, to inspire them to create new paintings and new musical compositions. The story deals with the relationships within the household and the conflicts that emerge when Luther and the couple's black cook, Mattie, fail to live up to the idealized (or arguably stereotyped) roles that Anne and Michael expect them to play.

As when reading most fiction, you may want to consider the role of the narrator in this particular story and whether or not the narrator seems neutral or biased. While the narrator may seem neutral at first, the details that the narrator provides subtly guide the reader to sympathize with Luther and Mattie just as it steers the reader to feel cynicism, if not something much worse, toward the white couple and to question their motivations. At least one critic, in fact, finds that "[t]he characterization of the White people in 'Slave on the Block' practically drips with irony" (Olmsted 73). As an active reader, you will want to be alert to how the story that you are reading seeks to shape your views of specific characters in the story. You may note, for example, that the story tells the reader repeatedly that the married white couple, particularly Anne, naively views blacks as a "[d]ear, natural childlike people" (32), as "simple and natural" (34), and as marked by "delightful simplicity" (34).

To write about "Slave on the Block," start with an engaged close reading of the story. Read for comprehension first. In your second and later readings, record your comments and reactions. Ask questions and make observations about themes and language, perhaps beginning with the opening description of the married couple in the story:

> They were people who went in for Negroes—Michael and Anne—the Carraways. But not in the social-service, philanthropic sort of way, no. They saw no use in helping a race that was already too charming and naïve and lovely for words. Leave them unspoiled and just enjoy them, Michael and Anne felt. (30)

How sincere and deep is the couple's interest in black people, for example? To what extent does their specific interest in black people determine what happens in the rest of the story? You may also be interested in analyzing the development (or lack of development) of the different characters in the story.

You may also note how the story presents the different reactions of the white and black individuals. The black characters remain mildly suspicious of their employers' motives, while the white couple (particularly Anne, the wife) seem to be at once fascinated by and firmly controlling of their black employees. Kate A. Baldwin offers an extensive discussion of the woman's conflicted idealization of and attraction to the young black man. The narrator also seems to avoid answering questions that might cause the reader to reevaluate her view of the black characters.

"Slave on the Block" can be viably discussed on its own or in the context of other literary and historical concerns. Hughes's story presents you with the opportunity to conduct outside research on related topics. For example, you may be interested in exploring the sudden interest of white intellectuals and artists in Harlem and in all things black during the Harlem Renaissance. Review the different topics and strategies in the following section for further ideas on how you might develop your paper idea more fully.

TOPICS AND STRATEGIES
Themes

Sample Topics:

1. **The ways of white folks:** Explore how the short story "Slave on the Block" develops the theme of white people's treatment (or mistreatment) of black people.

   The short story "Berry" is not one of the best works included in the volume *The Ways of White Folks*, but the story is noteworthy for containing the volume's title in a passage that captures the theme of the entire volume. The title character in "Berry" says at one point: "[T]he ways of white folks, I mean some white folks, is too much for me. I reckon they must be a few good ones, but most of 'em ain't good—leastwise they don't treat me good. And Lawd knows, I ain't never done nothin' to 'em, nothin' a-tall" (114). Reread "Slave on the Block," paying particular attention to the behaviors of the main characters, and explore whether or not Berry's observation applies equally to the married couple Michael and Anne Carraway, to Luther, and to other characters in "Slave on the Block."

2. **Continuity and change:** Analyze the short story "Slave on the Block" in terms of the theme of how much or how little white attitudes toward blacks have changed or have not changed in the United States from the time of slavery to the modern age.

   Details in the short story "Slave on the Block" suggest that the artistic white couple, who pride themselves on their intelligence and liberal thinking, remain entrenched in racist attitudes that can be traced back to slavery. For example, the art that they are inspired by Luther's presence to create, whether it be her paintings or his musical compositions, always has a slavery theme. Identify and analyze details in the story that will help you construct the argument that "Slave on the Block" demonstrates more continuity than radical change in the white attitudes toward blacks from the slavery era into the modern age.

3. **Black subjects in modern art:** Read Hughes's short story "Slave on the Block" as an invitation to explore the strong interest of many white artists and intellectuals of the early 20th century in all things "primitive."

The white artist couple's fascination with black people in Hughes's short story mirrors the strong interest of many early-20th-century artists, including such famous names as Pablo Picasso. Explore this centrality of black subjects in modern art or the white interest in black figures of the Harlem Renaissance, several of whom feature prominently in the story's opening paragraphs. In keeping with the theme of this short story, you may want to explore the less positive aspects of this interest in the "primitive."

4. **White patronage, condescension, segregation, and hypocrisy:** Analyze Hughes's treatment of the white patronage of black individuals in the short story "Slave on the Block." You may want to compare and contrast two or more of his short stories on this topic.

To develop a comparison and contrast essay that makes use of the short story "Slave on the Block," you may wish to read one or more of Hughes's other short stories that focus extensively on the white patronage of black individuals in the early 20th century, such as "Poor Little Black Fellow," "The Blues I'm Playing," and "Rejuvenation Through Joy." You may wish to focus at least part of your analysis on the similar, angry confrontations at the end of many of these stories. A strong essay on this topic will go beyond the particulars of each story and make a larger argument about Hughes's views of the patronage system that was so important to him and to many other artists of the Harlem Renaissance.

Form and Genre

Sample Topics:

1. **Form and structure of the story:** Identify and discuss the formal techniques through which the short story "Slave on the Block" is developed. In your discussion, consider the various

ways that you may analyze the form and structure of the story, including the story's use of narration, point of view, direct dialogue and summary dialogue, and conflict and resolution.

In *Langston Hughes: A Study of the Short Fiction,* Hans Ostrom writes that Hughes's stories are not experimentalist and are instead based on "simple narrative forms—the tale, the sketch, the parable, and deliberately undramatic reportage" (qtd. in *The Collected Works of Langston Hughes* 15:2). Explain whether or not you find that Ostrom's statement applies to the short story "Slave on the Block."

2. **Black folk speech and art forms in the story:** Write an essay exploring the level of success that Hughes has in incorporating black folk speech and art forms in the short story "Slave on the Block."

In *Langston Hughes: A Study of the Short Fiction,* Hans Ostrom writes that Hughes is "interested in allowing colloquial language, the blues, gospel music, and the sound and sense of 'street speech' to inform the language of his short fiction" (qtd. in *The Collected Works of Langston Hughes* 15:2). Identify places in the story in which these elements surface, including the colloquial speech and the song lyrics that appear in the story. To expand your subject for a more developed paper, consider discussing Hughes's use of black vernacular and black art forms in one or more of his other works or consider comparing Hughes with one of his Harlem Renaissance contemporaries who also wrote prose fiction, such as Zora Neale Hurston or Jessie Fauset.

3. **Guy de Maupassant and Langston Hughes:** Explore the short stories of the French author Guy de Maupassant to determine to what extent he might have served as an influence on Hughes.

In *The Big Sea,* Hughes identifies the French writer Guy de Maupassant as an important influence on him: "I think it was de Maupassant who made me really want to be a writer and write stories about Negroes, so true that people in far-away lands would read them—even after I was dead" (51). The influence may show itself in any number of places, such as in the content of the stories, in the themes that are developed, or in the narrative techniques of the stories.

Bibliography for "Slave on the Block"

Baldwin, Kate A. "The Russian Connection: Interracialism as Queer Alliance in *The Ways of White Folks.*" *Montage of a Dream: The Art and Life of Langston Hughes.* Ed. John Edgar Tidwell, Cheryl R. Ragar, and Arnold Rampersad. Columbia: U of Missouri P, 2007. 209–36.

Olmsted, Jane. "Black Moves, White Ways, Every Body's Blues: Orphic Power in Langston Hughes's *The Ways of White Folks.*" *Black Orpheus: Music in African American Fiction from the Harlem Renaissance to Toni Morrison.* Ed. Saadi A. Simawe. New York: Routledge, 2000. 65–89.

Ostrom, Hans. *Langston Hughes: A Study of the Short Fiction.* New York: Twayne, 1993.

NOT WITHOUT LAUGHTER

READING TO WRITE

MOST FIRST novels are heavily autobiographical, and Hughes's *Not Without Laughter* (1930) is no exception. In this work, Hughes traces the coming of age of James "Sandy" Rogers, a young black man who in many ways experiences a life that parallels that of Hughes. Many of the specific details differ: Sandy's shiftless father loves the blues and leaves at the novel's end to fight in World War I, while Hughes's own hardworking father has no patience for black folk culture and lives in Mexico while Hughes is growing up. Nonetheless, the larger parallels are strong and compelling. Like Hughes, to name just a few examples, Sandy grows up in a small midwestern town in the early decades of the 20th century and later moves to Chicago, has limited contact with his biological parents, and begins writing in high school.

In his later autobiographical work *The Big Sea*, Hughes explains that he ran into difficulties when trying to transform his own life experiences into fiction:

> I wanted to write about a typical Negro family in the Middle West, about people like those I had known in Kansas. But mine was not a typical Negro family. My grandmother never took in washing or worked in service or went much to church. She had lived in Oberlin and spoke perfect English, without a trace of dialect. She looked like an Indian. My mother was a newspaper woman and a stenographer then. My father lived in Mexico City. My granduncle had been a congressman. And there were

heroic memories of John Brown's raid and the underground railroad in the family storehouse.

But I thought maybe I had been a typical Negro boy. I grew up with the other Negro children of Lawrence, sons and daughters of family friends. I had an uncle of sorts who ran a barber shop in Kansas City. And later a stepfather who was a wanderer. We were poor—but different. For purposes of the novel, however, I created around myself what seemed to me a family more typical of Negro life in Kansas than my own had been. I gave myself aunts that I didn't have, modeled after other children's aunts whom I had known. But I put in a real cyclone that had blown my grandmother's porch away. And I added dances and songs I remembered. I brought the boy to Chicago in his teens, as I had come to Chicago—but I did not leave behind a well-fixed aunt whose husband was a mail clerk. (228)

Thus, one notable element of the novel is the way in which Hughes alters substantial elements in his own biography in order to create a story that seems to him more "typical of Negro life" at the time. In doing so, Hughes adds many elements to the story that allow his fictional family to become a microcosm of black life in the early 20th century. In a more general sense, this story of the fate of three generations of one family comes to represent the generational conflicts between the old and the new, including the religious and the secular, as well as the weight of history and the promise of radical change. For example, Aunt Hager was born to an African slave, grew up in slavery, and still enjoys retelling the "[s]lavery-time stories, myths, folktales" (129). However, her three daughters seek to improve their lot in life by making a clean break with the past; all three end up moving northward, following the general trend of the Great Migration of black Americans in the early 20th century. Further, through these three younger women and their different personalities and goals, Hughes is able to capture a range of black American experience. One daughter seeks to assimilate to the standards of the dominant white culture, while another leaves home to follow her husband in the North, and a third nurtures her dislike of white people and pursues a career as a blues singer.

In its frequent discussions of the blues and its incorporation of blues lyrics, *Not Without Laughter* features one of the dominant themes in

Hughes's works, the celebration of black folk art, particularly the forms of black music and black vernacular English. For some readers, the novel is at its best when the narrator forgets the story and simply, directly, and lovingly presents these elements of black culture, particularly examples of the intimate culture of black men as is found in the jokes, boasts, and friendly games of insults in several carefully described and developed settings in the novel, including a men's washroom at a high school dance, a barber shop, and a pool hall. In these settings, the storytelling seems almost to come to a halt, and the author's delight in black (male) folk culture takes over, as suggested in Hughes's use of a phrase in chapter 25, the chapter centering on the all-male space of the pool hall, as the title of the novel.

A second theme broached in the novel that is common (although far less important than folk expression) to Hughes's writing is the attempt to make sense of which of the two great race leaders of the late 19th and early 20th centuries, Booker T. Washington and W. E. B. Du Bois, with their different views on how to achieve racial equality, would most benefit blacks in America. In the novel, this conflict is represented by the way two women in Sandy's life talk about the two men. His grandmother Aunt Hager speaks in worshipful tones of Washington and embodies in her daily life his emphasis on hard work and loyal service to white employers and white neighbors. Sandy's Aunt Tempy represents the other extreme, dismissing Washington as "some white folks' nigger" (171) and praising Du Bois's emphasis on education and high culture. The chapter in this volume on the poem "Ballad of Booker T." explores Hughes's changing views toward these race leaders in more detail, and a strong essay could result from discussing the connections between the novel and the poem.

The writing of the novel itself has an interesting history that is worthy of additional exploration. In one section of *The Big Sea*, Hughes presents himself as the solitary, creative artist as he details his frustrations with drafting and revising the novel alone in his dormitory room; he writes that he began the novel in his junior year in college, continued to work on it as a senior, and saw it reach print the next year (228). In a later section of the autobiography, however, he provides a fuller picture of the situation and explains that it was only possible for him to write the novel because of the extensive financial and material support that he received from his white patron, Charlotte Mason. Mason also "read both drafts of it, had helped me with it, and found it good" (235). This patronage may have not come without a cost, however. At least two critics, Thomas H. Nigel and John P. Shields, explore this subject in detail. Shields examines sections of early drafts of the novel that did not find their way into the final version and argues that Mason's influence may have prevented him from producing "the novel that Hughes intended to write" and may have forced him "to suppress his increasingly strong left-wing political notions in the novel" (601). One of the sections that did not find its way into the finished novel, as related by Shields, is an extensive description of worship practices at a black revival meeting. Still, the influence of the excised section's presence in an early draft of the novel is likely to be sensed by the careful reader, who may detect the overlap of two musical forms—one religious and one secular—in several passages in the novel. One such passage opens chapter 9 of the novel, titled "Carnival":

> Between the tent of Christ and the tents of sin there stretched scarcely a half-mile. Rivalry reigned: the revival and the carnival held sway in Stanton at the same time. Both were at the south edge of town, and both were loud and musical in their activities . . . and after sundown these August evenings the mourning songs of the Christians could be heard rising from the Hickory Woods while the profound syncopation of the minstrel band blared from Galoway's Lots, strangely intermingling their notes of praise and joy. (82)

A second, briefer passage in the next chapter of the novel recycles material from the carnival chapter as a set of condensed images from Sandy's dreams: "he would awaken suddenly from dreaming that he heard sad raggy music playing while a woman shouted for Jesus in the Gospel tent" (90).

As is the case with most or all novels, *Not Without Laughter* presents a wide range of possible subjects for writing. You may have difficulty writing a focused, unified paper unless you work to settle on a clear topic and limit your discussion to items that are closely related to that focus. Review the different topics and strategies in the following section for ideas on how you might develop and strengthen your analysis of some aspect of the novel. The novel is not difficult to read and has little to none of the formal experimentation (such as stream-of-consciousness or radical shifts in perspective) that was becoming commonplace in literature by the 1930s. Having chosen a topic or set of related topics for your paper, you may want to read some or all of the novel a second time in order to identify important passages and developments that will fit meaningfully into your discussion and analysis.

TOPICS AND STRATEGIES
Character

Sample Topics:

1. **Jimboy as fantasized father:** Analyze the character of Sandy's father, Jimboy, in the novel *Not Without Laughter.*

   Comb the novel for details about the character Jimboy. Perhaps focus on aspects of his family background and on his view of blues music and other elements of black culture. In a longer and more developed essay, you may want to contrast Hughes's presentation of this fictional father with his presentation of his real father in the opening section of *The Big Sea.*

2. **Tempy and trying to be white:** Analyze the character of Sandy's Aunt Tempy in the novel *Not Without Laughter.*

   What details does the novel present about the character Tempy? Focus on her views on black vernacular English, folk culture and high culture, and black-white race relations. Alternately, you could compare Hughes's presentation of this fictional aunt with his criticism of blacks trying to be white in his early essay "The Negro Artist and the Racial Mountain."

History and Context

Sample Topics:

1. **Black life in the early decades of the twentieth century:** Identify and research the details presented in the novel *Not Without Laughter* that help one more fully understand the living conditions for black people in the early 20th century.

   As always, you will want to read carefully; details in *Not Without Laughter* that reveal aspects of black life in the early decades of the 20th century may be found in unsuspected places. For example,

Jimboy's first letter in the novel, dated 1912, contains his observations that there are limited employment opportunities for blacks and that blacks must compete with newly arrived immigrants for jobs. Later in the novel, Sister Johnson tells a story of a race riot, with homes burned and black people forced to leave the town out of fear for their lives. Researching either topic—employment opportunities or race riots—is likely to lead to interesting papers on history and context. A third possibility for writing a paper on this topic would be to explore the novel's connections to other, more general historical developments, such as the Great Migration of blacks northward in the early 20th century.

2. **African Americans in World War I:** Use selected details that are presented in the novel *Not Without Laughter* as an invitation to explore how many black Americans viewed the war.

The novel makes multiple, albeit brief references to Jimboy's participation in World War I, presents a substantial discussion of Tempy's hope that black participation and sacrifice in the war will improve race relations at home, and drops a hint through Harriet that at least some blacks saw World War I as "this white folks' war" (207). Consider developing this topic more fully by exploring other published statements on black views on the war, such as W.E.B. Du Bois's short essay "Returning Soldiers" as well as online resources such as the Library of Congress's online exhibition *The African American Odyssey: A Quest for Full Citizenship* (particularly the section titled "World War I and Postwar Society"), National Public Radio's account of a recently discovered diary of a black soldier in World War I, and the EDSITEment lesson plan titled "African-American Soldiers After World War I: Had Race Relations Changed?" These online resources are cited at the end of this chapter.

Form and Genre

Sample Topics:
1. **Blues and gospel music:** Both forms of music, the blues and gospel, feature prominently in Hughes's novel *Not Without Laughter.* Explore their significance in the story.

With all its talk of the songs performed at revival meetings and in blues clubs and with two of its central characters—Aunt Hager and Jimboy—disagreeing over which form of music is better, the novel offers ample opportunity to explore these two forms of music and to discuss their importance to the work overall. You may wish to extend your discussion beyond the novel and address, more generally, how the two forms of music are not entirely unrelated yet are often seen as mutually exclusive. You may also be interested in reviewing Hughes's published statements and treatments of these musical forms, as seen for example in his essay "The Negro Artist and the Racial Mountain," the short story "The Blues I'm Playing," and the novel *Tambourines to Glory*.

2. **Bildungsroman:** Explore the extent to which Hughes's first novel *Not without Laughter* can be seen as a bildungsroman, a story of informal education and of the transition from childhood into adulthood.

You may wish to review definitions and discussions of the term *bildungsroman* and form your own list of elements in the book that seem to reflect or borrow from the bildungsroman tradition. You may wish to review particular scenes in the novel that seem to signal Sandy's emerging understanding of adult concerns, including but not limited to sexual desire. Consider also how seemingly minor details, such as Sandy's experience being called "Mr. Rogers" for the first time in his life in one of the closing chapters (199), may hint at some of the meaningful but abstract developments in the novel.

Language, Symbols, and Imagery

Sample Topics:

1. **Nature:** Explore Sandy's connection to or alienation from nature in the novel *Not Without Laughter.*

The natural world figures prominently in the chapters of *Not without Laughter* that are set in the small Kansas town of

Stanton during Sandy's childhood but is conspicuously absent in the later chapters, when Sandy goes to live with his mother in Chicago. You may wish to explore this or other treatments of the natural world in the novel. You may want to read one or more published explorations of this topic, such as Elizabeth Schultz's essay "Natural and Unnatural Circumstances in *Not without Laughter.*"

2. **Brass spittoons:** Compare and contrast Hughes's use of the symbol of the brass spittoon to discuss the relationship between the black worker and white employer in two of his works, the novel *Not Without Laughter* and the poem "Brass Spittoons."

In chapter 20 of *Not Without Laughter,* Sandy takes on an after-school job, cleaning the six large brass spittoons at the Drummer's Hotel in his hometown of Stanton, Kansas. Contrast Sandy's position toward these objects with the implied position of the unnamed worker in four American cities in Hughes's poem "Brass Spittoons." Work to establish strong points of commonality or difference between the two pieces, such as reflecting on both the phrase "Hey, boy!" and the implicit or explicit racism that appears in both pieces. A related topic would be the exploration of the job of elevator boy as described in chapter 29 of *Not Without Laughter* and in the poem "Elevator Boy." Attempt to address both poems and their connections to the novel. In a more developed essay on this topic, you may want to conclude with a reflection on the term *intertexuality* (the connections and relations among different literary works) and its presence and significance in Hughes's writings.

Compare and Contrast Essays

Sample Topics:

1. **Religious and hardworking black women:** Compare and contrast Aunt Hager in the novel *Not Without Laughter* and Essie in the novel *Tambourines to Glory.*

In *A Historical Guide to Langston Hughes,* Steven C. Tracy writes that Hughes "emerges as a black male feminist" because of his sympathetic focus on the social conditions and challenges of black women (123). In his discussion of this point, he focuses part of his discussion on Hughes's representations of religious and hardworking black women in his writings. In addition to the two novels, there are other, shorter works by Hughes that you may wish to review and possibly include in your analysis, such as the poems "The Negro Mother," "Prayer Meeting," "Southern Mammy Sings," and "Spirituals."

2. **Small town versus big city:** Describe and discuss the different settings in Hughes's novels *Not Without Laughter* and *Tambourines to Glory.*

Make note of the significant differences in the settings of Hughes's two novels *Not Without Laughter* and *Tambourines to Glory* and explore the impact of those settings on the characters' lives. The first novel is set in a Kansas town with a mixed population of whites and blacks, for example, while the second is set in Harlem and features few white characters. In both cases, the setting establishes a number of elements in the story, including what sorts of opportunities for employment are available. You may be interested in focusing on the different social networks in the two novels, perhaps contrasting the well-established social "lodge" in *Not Without Laughter* with the makeshift storefront church of *Tambourines to Glory.* Another possible focus for an essay on this topic would be to reflect on the status of particular characters within their communities. You may wish to discuss whether they are fully integrated and valued members of their community, for example, or whether they suffer from anonymity and limited social networks and support systems.

3. **Real and imagined fathers:** Compare and contrast Hughes's presentation of two very different father figures, his own father in the autobiography *The Big Sea* and Sandy's father in the novel *Not Without Laughter.*

In analyzing the different father figures in *The Big Sea* and *Not Without Laughter,* you may wish to focus on the fathers' views of art, time, and black people in general. This topic may lead to a compelling paper in which you show how in his novel *Not Without Laughter* Hughes may be creating for himself the positive father figure that he had never had as a young man.

Bibliography and Online Resources for *Not Without Laughter*

"African-American Soldiers After World War I: Had Race Relations Changed?" EDSITEment. National Endowment for the Humanities. http://edsitement. neh.gov/view_lesson_plan.asp?id=498

Chasar, Mike. "The Sounds of Black Laughter and the Harlem Renaissance: Claude McKay, Sterling Brown, Langston Hughes." *American Literature: A Journal of Literary History, Criticism, and Bibliography* 80.1 (March 2008): 57–81.

"Diary Provides Black Soldier's View of WWI." npr.org. http://www.npr.org/ templates/story/story.php?storyId=3178013#commentBlock

Du Bois, W.E.B. "Returning Soldiers." *The Portable Harlem Renaissance Reader.* Ed. David Levering Lewis. New York: Penguin, 1995. 3–5.

Kiesel, Linda R. *"Like a Stream of Living Faith": The Folklore in Langston Hughes's Not Without Laughter.* Chapel Hill: U of North Carolina P, 1982.

Langston Hughes in Lawrence: 1902–1915. http://www.continuinged.ku.edu/ hughes/files_city/index.html

Langston Hughes on the Map of Kansas Literature. http://www.washburn.edu/ reference/cks/mapping/hughes/index.html

Nigel, Thomas H. "Patronage and the Writing of Langston Hughes's *Not Without Laughter:* A Paradoxical Case." *CLA Journal* 42.1 (Sept. 1998): 48–70.

"Not Without Laughter and Other Recent Fiction." *New York Times.* August 3, 1930. http://www.nytimes.com/books/01/04/22/specials/hughes-notwithout.html

Schultz, Elizabeth. "Natural and Unnatural Circumstances in *Not Without Laughter." Montage of a Dream: The Art and Life of Langston Hughes.* Ed. John Edgar Tidwell, Cheryl R. Ragar, and Arnold Rampersad. Columbia: U of Missouri P, 2007. 39–51.

Shields, John P. "'Never Cross the Divide': Reconstructing Langston Hughes's *Not Without Laughter." African American Review* 28.4 (Winter 1994): 601–13.

Tracy, Steven C. *A Historical Guide to Langston Hughes.* New York: Oxford UP, 2004.

Wall, Cheryl A. "Whose Sweet Angel Child? Blues Women, Langston Hughes, and Writing During the Harlem Renaissance." *GRAAT: Publication des*

Groupes de Recherches Anglo-Américaines de l'Université François Rabelais de Tours 14 (1996): 63–72.

"World War I and Postwar Society" *The African American Odyssey: A Quest for Full Citizenship,* Library of Congress. http://lcweb2.loc.gov/ammem/aaohtml/exhibit/aopart7.html

TAMBOURINES
TO GLORY

READING TO WRITE

HUGHES'S SECOND, much shorter novel, *Tambourines to Glory* (1958), was first written as a play, a fact that perhaps explains why the novel is particularly easy and enjoyable to read. *Tambourines to Glory* is structured as a series of 36 chapters, some measuring barely more than a page in length, and is heavy on dialogue but light on the devices that are commonly expected in modern novels, such as elaborate external descriptions or lengthy internal monologues.

The setting of *Tambourines to Glory* is the black community of Harlem in New York City sometime in the early 1950s. The exact years are never stated, but the story is clearly set in the post–World War II era, with glancing references to the atom bomb and the Korean War as well as brief mentions of famous religious and artistic personalities such as Billy Graham, Doc Wheeler, and Eartha Kitt. The actual cast of characters in the novel is fairly small, and the story centers on two poor, longtime friends, Essie Belle Johnson and Laura Wright Reed, and their efforts to establish a new church in Harlem. The Reed Sisters, as they come to call themselves, have tremendous success, quickly moving from street corner to storefront to renovated theater. With the success of their enterprise, however, come increasingly powerful temptations to abuse their newfound wealth and influence. Thus, *Tambourines to Glory* allows Hughes to explore one of his favorite subjects, the shortcomings (and perhaps even shams) of organized religion. Early in the novel, for example, Hughes names and criticizes two important religious leaders—Aimee Semple McPherson and George Wilson Becton—whom he criticizes in several of his other writings (see, for example, the discussions of religion in the chapters in this volume on "Goodbye Christ" and *The Big Sea*). Much of the rest of the novel, particularly the parts detailing the increasingly predatory and greed-driven actions of Laura and Big-Eyed Buddy Loman, can certainly be read as Hughes's own sustained critique of organized religion that becomes a money-making enterprise.

In his book-length study *Langston Hughes: The Man, His Art, and His Continuing Influence*, C. James Trotman addresses Hughes's ability to remain passionately interested in spirituals and gospel music but largely uninterested in or openly critical of organized religion:

> The fact that Hughes could throw one arm around spirituals and gospel music and the other arm around the blues simultaneously would seem remarkable, even blasphemous, in some circles, primarily Christian ones where the blues might be dubbed "the devil's music." But Hughes sat them rather comfortably side by side in his work and his ethos. "I like the barrel houses of Seventh Street, the shouting churches, and the songs," he wrote in *The Big Sea* (209); the following year he called spirituals and blues the "two great Negro gifts to American music" ("Songs Called the Blues," 143). In the mid-fifties his devil figure Big Eye Buddy Lomax [sic], in both the play and the novel *Tambourines to Glory*, asserted that "them gospel songs sound just like the blues," to which the holy sister managed only the feeble reply, "At least our words is different" (*Tambourines*, 126–27). (53)

Readers may disagree with Trotman's characterization of Essie's reply to Buddy as "feeble," but the novel presents a view consistent with one of Hughes's central interests, the inherent beauty of all forms of contemporary black American popular culture, whether religious or secular. In this novel, more so than in some of his other works, Hughes is perhaps on his best behavior and seems most able to praise something even as he criticizes it.

At the same time, the novel allows Hughes to treat a broader range of themes, such as the tension between the promise and the reality of life for blacks in northern urban centers. In chapter 21 of *Tambourines to*

Glory, for example, Essie's daughter Marietta arrives from "down South" by bus to join her mother in Harlem. This chapter begins with what is for this novel an unusually long narration:

> Wonderland of the North—where white folks and colored folks all sit anywhere on a bus. The North where you can be colored and still get a Coca-Cola in any drugstore without having to carry it outside to drink it. The North—where young folks all go to school together. The North where New York is, Chicago, Detroit—and Harlem.
>
> They all had come originally from the South—Essie, Laura, Buddy, plus just about everybody else in their church, too. Mighty magnet of the colored race—the North! Roll bus! Roll across that Jim Crow River called the Potomac! Roll past the white dome of the Capitol! Roll down the New Jersey Turnpike, through the Holland Tunnel and up and out from under the river into the North! New York! Roll into the magic streets of Manhattan! Harlem, a chocolate ice cream cone in New York's white napkin. (280)

At first glance, this passage may seem wholly positive, praising the move by African Americans from the South to the North as an act of deliverance from dehumanizing segregation, perhaps even as a modernized version of escape from slavery into freedom via the Underground Railroad. Yet the details presented in *Tambourines to Glory* about the living and working conditions for black Americans in Harlem paint a different, far less positive picture. This passage about emerging onto the "magic streets of Manhattan" may contain at least as much irony as it does conviction.

As is the case with most or all novels, *Tambourines to Glory* presents a wide range of possible subjects to discuss and explore. You may have difficulty writing a focused, unified essay unless you work to settle on a clear topic and limit your discussion to items that are closely related to that topic. Review the different topics and strategies in the following section for ideas on how you might develop and focus your analysis of some aspect of the novel. Having chosen a topic or set of related topics for your paper, you may want to read the novel a second time in order to identify important passages and developments in the novel that will fit meaningfully into your discussion and analysis. Because the novel has received little critical attention, you will find a great deal of opportunity for original research and writing on *Tambourines to Glory* and, indeed, may want to view yourself as breaking new ground in your paper.

TOPICS AND STRATEGIES
Themes
Sample Topics:

1. **Capitalizing on Christ:** Explore the treatment of commercialized Christianity in the novel *Tambourines to Glory.*

In writing an essay on this topic, you might draw on cultural and historical studies of Christianity in the early decades of the 20th century, preferably books by university presses or other reputable publishers. Consider devoting at least part of the essay to a discussion of two evangelical leaders denounced in the opening of the novel, Aimee Semple McPherson and George Wilson Becton. For information on McPherson, look to Matthew Avery Sutton's book *Aimee Semple McPherson and the Resurrection of Christian America.* For information on Becton, review Hughes's detailed discussion of him in the "Spectacles in Color" section of *The Big Sea* (13: 210–12) as well as the entry on him in *The Encyclopedia of the Harlem Renaissance.* (In reading about Becton and McPherson, you may discover strong parallels between these real religious figures and the fictional Reed Sisters. Among the parallels between Becton and the Reed Sisters, for example, you may note that the soft glowing cross observed by Hughes in Becton's chambers in *The Big Sea* seems much like the lighted one hanging on the wall in the living room of Essie and Laura's new uptown apartment in chapter 21 of *Tambourines to Glory.*) For a more general discussion of Christianity in early-20th-century America, perhaps read the introductory essay and review some of the documents relevant to the time period in Milton Sernett's *African American Religious History: A Documentary Witness.* Alternately, you might use Hughes's novel as an opportunity to examine the commercialization of religion in contemporary American society. A possible source for this topic might be William Connoll's *Capitalism and Christianity, American Style.* A variation on this topic might be to explore Hughes's writings over the course of his career to search for evidence of what Harold Bloom calls the author's "lifelong suspicion of religion" (53), a sentiment presented, among other places, in his earlier poem "Goodbye Christ" and in his autobiographical work *The Big Sea.* In order to develop a strong argument of your own, consider exploring the possibility that Hughes's position toward religion does not remain constant throughout his life.

2. **Brownskin angels and white devils:** Use Laura's instructions to the artist in chapter 11 in the novel *Tambourines to Glory* as an invitation to explore the problem of how to represent God, angels, and the devil in human form.

In chapter 11 of *Tambourines to Glory,* Laura instructs the artist to paint dark-skinned angels, a God who is "black, or at least dark brown," and a white devil (252). This topic can be taken in any number of directions. You may be interested in exploring how Laura is seeking here to counter the representations of the divine and the infernal in dominant American culture, for example, or you could explore how Laura's language (particularly the idea of white devils) echoes some of the teaching of the Nation of Islam by the 1950s. A third option would be to approach the notion of a "white devil" more as a metaphor and explore how Hughes's novel in particular presents white people (ranging from a local police officer on the beat to the mysterious Marty, "the fixer, the man behind the men *behind* the men," 264) who have power, are predatory, and corrupt whatever they touch.

Character

Sample Topics:

1. **Essie and Laura:** Compare and contrast Essie Belle Johnson and Laura Wright Reed, the two main characters in the novel *Tambourines to Glory.*

From the opening chapters, the novel *Tambourines to Glory* sets up explicit and implicit contrasts but also meaningful connections between the two main characters. While some of these differences are purely physical in nature (one character is physically attractive, the other is not), the most interesting points of difference probably address questions of motivation and conviction in their shared enterprise of founding a new church. You may find one character much more sympathetic or admirable than the other, but in the course of your analysis of the two characters, you may also decide that, while one may be more idealistic than the other, both have redeemable qualities and both have their own failings. To explore the connections, you may want to explore what the two women share in their lives, and you may even find yourself questioning Laura's assertion, using a popular biblical allusion, that they have no deep connection between them toward the end of the novel: "Girl, you ain't Ruth, and I ain't Naomi" (293).

2. **The devil figure:** Explore how the character Big-Eyed Buddy Loman plays the role of the devil (or the devil's henchman) in the novel *Tambourines to Glory.*

In a passage quoted in the opening section of this chapter, C. James Trotman identifies Big-Eyed Buddy Loman as Hughes's "devil figure" in the novel. Make a case for the accuracy or inaccuracy of this characterization of Buddy. You may want to focus in particular on his role as tempter or corruptor. You may also want to consider how the few details that the reader is given about Buddy—such as his enormous hands or his skill at playing blues music—may be seen as contributing to his ability to tempt or corrupt.

History and Context

Sample Topics:

1. **Urban black life in the 1950s:** Use Hughes's representation of urban black life in the novel *Tambourines to Glory* as an invitation to explore the challenges of being black and poor and living in Harlem in the 1950s.

Draw out the details in the novel *Tambourines to Glory* that speak to the living conditions of Essie and Laura. For example, answer some or all of the following questions: How large are their two apartments, particularly the ones that they occupy at the beginning of the novel? What sort of view do they have from their windows? Who are the other residents? How do they make a living? For one detailed discussion of the transformation of Harlem from mecca to ghetto by the 1950s, see James De Jongh's book-length study *Vicious Modernism: Black Harlem and the Literary Imagination,* particularly the opening of the section "The Emerging Ghetto: The 1940s and 1950s." You will want to focus on Harlem whenever possible, but you may find it helpful to discuss other black urban centers, including enclaves in Chicago and Detroit. If you would like to include discussions of other literary works from the same period that also deal with black urban life, poverty, and small living spaces, you may want to look at Gwendolyn Brooks's poem "Kitchenette Building" and Lorraine Hansberry's play *A Raisin in the Sun.*

2. **The Great Migration:** Research the mass migration of African Americans northward in the early decades of the 20th century and apply some of the knowledge that you have gained to a closer reading of the novel *Tambourines to Glory.*

You may wish to begin with an analysis of the passage from *Tambourines to Glory* quoted in the opening section of this chapter (beginning "Wonderland of the North") and a consideration of how well this hopeful, perhaps blindly idealistic description of the life waiting for black Americans in Harlem and other northern urban centers matches or fails to match actual, lived experiences in the North. An essay on this topic either can focus on the evidence provided within the novel or can draw on secondary sources detailing the realities of life in 1950s Harlem, such as James De Jongh's study *Vicious Modernism: Black Harlem and the Literary Imagination.*

Form and Genre

Sample Topics:

1. **Play and novel:** Explore the similarities and differences between the play and novel versions of *Tambourines to Glory* and, when possible, consider how these differences may be tied to the differences in the genres themselves.

   While this topic may result in a simple and successful comparison and contrast essay, you may find it more interesting and challenging to explore how some or all of the differences may be related to the two genres involved. Plays and novels are different, after all, and one expects the two to emphasize different aspects even when telling the same story. Consider, for example, the use of narration in the novel and the use of stage directions in the play. A beginning point for secondary reading might be the brief discussion of the "Scenic Method" in the student guide *"Tambourines to Glory,* Langston Hughes, 1958." If you use this source, of course, you will want to develop further ideas and examples of your own.

2. **Gospel music:** Explore the significance of the gospel lyrics that are presented directly to the reader in nearly every chapter of the novel *Tambourines to Glory.*

   The gospel music that appears in nearly every chapter of *Tambourines to Glory* may serve one or more purposes throughout the novel. These songs may be purely for entertainment or show, may express true convictions, or may have multiple and even ironic layers of meaning. (The latter may be the case, for example, in chapter 31, when Sister Birdie Lee first witnesses a murder and then, only minutes later, is singing and shouting in church that she will "witness" and "testify" before the gathered crowd.) You may be interested in reviewing the brief section "Gospel Music" in the student guide *"Tambourines to Glory,* Langston Hughes, 1958." If you use this source, of course, you will want to develop further ideas and examples of your own.

Language, Symbols, and Imagery

Sample Topics:

1. **Foreshadowing:** Explore the use of foreshadowing in the novel *Tambourines to Glory*.

You may want to review the concepts informing the use of foreshadowing. Your examination is likely to focus at least initially on Essie's knife, which appears early in the story and is mentioned repeatedly throughout the chapters until finally used for dramatic effect toward the end of the novel. Evaluate how well Hughes employs the knife as a device throughout the novel. In the course of your reading and thinking about the structure of *Tambourines to Glory,* you may find other, more subtle literary techniques. A beginning point for secondary reading and for developing a more nuanced discussion might be the brief section on "Foreshadowing" in the student guide "*Tambourines to Glory,* Langston Hughes, 1958."

2. **Dialect and diction:** Explore the full range of African-American speaking styles in the novel *Tambourines to Glory.*

The novel *Tambourines to Glory* opens with a sharp contrast between the standard English of the narrator and the lively vernacular of Essie and Laura, and throughout the novel there are widely varying varieties of English that could make for a rich topic of discussion for an essay. In addition to looking at the speech of Essie and Laura, you may also want to contrast the street slang of Big-Eyed Buddy Loman with the mainstream, educated speech of the unnamed "refined" artist in chapter 11 (the word *refined* is used at least twice in the novel, in very similar contexts, and probably serves here as a code term for gay) and of CJ, the clean-cut "gospel boy" of chapter 22. To develop your essay more fully, you may want to explore to what extent these speech patterns match current descriptions of black vernacular English or to discuss how quickly slang becomes dated. A beginning point for secondary reading might be the brief section on "Dialect and Diction" in "*Tambourines to Glory,* Langston Hughes, 1958."

3. **Religious symbols:** Identify several concrete items in the novel *Tambourines to Glory* that are connected with the newly founded church of the Reed Sisters and explore the possible larger, symbolic meanings of one or more of these items.

Three possible items (among others, no doubt) in *Tambourines to Glory* that may serve as symbols are the painting of Adam and Eve at the back of the storefront church, the gilded Bible, and the tambourine. Like all symbols, these items can be multivalent, meaning that they can convey multiple, even contradictory meanings at once. For example, in an essay cited at the end of this chapter, Joyce Hart observes that the tambourine in the novel serves both as an instrument of worship and as a collection plate and explores how this dualism of the tambourine matches the dualism of the two women, Essie and Laura, with their different goals for the church. You may wish to develop Hart's idea more fully or take a similar approach with another item and explore, for example, how Essie and Laura see different things even when looking at the same item, such as the wall painting or the gilded Bible. You may also wish to look at the statement made about religious symbols in general in chapter 20 of the novel.

Compare and Contrast Essays
Sample Topics:
1. **Harlem as mecca or as ghetto:** Explore Hughes's changing representations of Harlem in the novel *Tambourines to Glory* and in one or more of his other works over the course of his career.

Like many writers of the Harlem Renaissance in the 1920s, Hughes wrote early pieces that present a largely positive view of the vibrant all-black community of Harlem in New York City. As the bloom began to fade in Harlem, however, so too did Hughes change how he represented the community. For one detailed discussion of the transformation of Harlem from mecca to ghetto by the 1950s, see James De Jongh's book-length study *Vicious Modernism: Black Harlem and the Literary Imagination,* particularly the opening of the section "The Emerging Ghetto: The 1940s and 1950s." For an earlier, idealistic presentation of Harlem, you may wish to review the online copy of the 1925 *Survey Graphic* issue that showcased Harlem as the "Mecca of the New Negro." For equally vibrant but more critical views of Harlem by the later Hughes, you may want to look at his poems in the collection *Montage of a Dream Deferred.*

2. **Religious and nurturing black women:** Compare and contrast Aunt Hager in the novel *Not Without Laughter* and Essie in the novel *Tambourines to Glory.*

In *A Historical Guide to Langston Hughes,* Steven C. Tracy writes that Hughes "emerges as a black male feminist" because of his sympathetic focus on the social conditions and challenges of black women (123). In his discussion of this point, he focuses in part on Hughes's representations of religious and hardworking black women in his writings. In addition to the two novels, there are other, shorter works by Hughes that you may wish to review and possibly include in your analysis, such as the poems "The Negro Mother," "Prayer Meeting," "Southern Mammy Sings," and "Spirituals."

3. **Small town versus big city:** Describe and discuss the different settings in Hughes's novels *Not Without Laughter* and *Tambourines to Glory.*

Make note of the significant differences in the settings of Hughes's two novels *Not Without Laughter* and *Tambourines to Glory,* and explore the impact of those settings on the characters' lives. The first novel is set in a Kansas town with a mixed population of whites and blacks, while the second is set in Harlem and features few white characters. In both cases, the setting establishes a number of elements in the story, including what sorts of opportunities for employment are available. You may be interested in focusing on the different social networks presented in the two novels, perhaps contrasting the well-established social "lodge" in *Not Without Laughter* with the makeshift, storefront church of *Tambourines to Glory*. Another possible focus for an essay on this topic would be to explore the status of particular characters within their communities. You may wish to discuss whether these characters are fully integrated and valued members of their communities, for example, or whether they suffer from anonymity and limited social networks and support systems.

4. **Literature versus folklore:** Develop an argument as to whether or not the novel *Tambourines to Glory* is a work of literature or a collection of folklore.

Leroi Jones's provocative contemporary review of the novel *Tambourines to Glory* asserts that the novel demonstrates how Hughes is less a writer of literature and more a black folklorist. The novel *Tambourines to Glory* fails to achieve the status of literature, Jones argues in this review, because Hughes is "merely relying on the strength and vitality of that [black folk] tradition" to sustain the work and shows himself to be unable or unwilling "to extend the beauty or meaning of that tradition into a 'universal' statement" (287). Engaging a provocative statement such as this one can be a challenging and interesting way to begin your paper. You will want to read Jones's full review carefully, making sense of his distinctions between folklore and literature, and identifying his main assertions about the shortcomings of Hughes as a writer in general and of the novel *Tambourines to Glory* in particular. After working through the short review and checking Jones's assertions against your own understanding of the novel and its author, you will be in a good position to write a paper that agrees or disagrees with some or all of Jones's main points in his review.

Bibliography and Online Resources for *Tambourines to Glory*

Bloom, Harold, ed. *Langston Hughes*. Broomall, Penn.: Chelsea House, 1999.

De Jongh, James. *Vicious Modernism: Black Harlem and the Literary Imagination*. New York: Cambridge UP, 1990.

"Harlem: Mecca of the New Negro." *Survey Graphic*. March 1925. http://etext. virginia.edu/harlem/. 3 November 1996. Downloaded on February 26, 2009.

Hart, Joyce. Critical Essay on *Tambourines to Glory*. *Novels for Students*. Vol. 21. Detroit: Thomson Gale, 2005. 282-85.

Jones, Leroi. *"Tambourines to Glory."* *The Jazz Review* 2 (June 1959): 33–34. *"Tambourines to Glory,* Langston Hughes, 1958." *Novels for Students*. Vol. 21. Ed. Ira Milne and Timothy Sisler. Detroit: Thomson Gale, 2005. 286–89.

Sanders, Leslie Catherine. "'I've Wrestled with Them All My Life': Langston Hughes's *Tambourines to Glory*." *Black American Literature Forum* 25.1 (Spring 1991): 63–72.

"Tambourines to Glory, Langston Hughes, 1958." *Novels for Students*. Vol. 21. Ed. Ira Milne and Timothy Sisler. Detroit: Thomson Gale, 2005.

Trotman, C. James, ed. *Langston Hughes: The Man, His Art and His Continuing Influence*. New York: Garland, 1995.

INDEX

accuracy, quotations and 35
Adventures of Huckleberry Finn,
   (Twain) 8
"Advertisement for the Waldorf-
   Astoria" 72
Africa, different views of 86
African Americans
   class divisions among 97
   early 20th-century life of 172–173
   urban black life in the 1950s 184–
   185
   World War I and 173
*Afro-American Poetics: Revisions of
   Harlem and the Black Aesthetic*
   (Baker) 64
Afrocentrism 68, 88–89
age, of readers 67–68
"America" (Whitfield) 72
angels and devils, artistic depictions of
   183
art and artists
   artistic freedom and responsibility
   60
   black artists and 97–98
   brownskin angels and white devils
   183
   characters 60, 61
   compare and contrast essays 73,
   75–76
   folklore and 70
   "The Negro Artist and the Racial
   Mountain" 131–132
As I Lay Dying 13–16
audiences, different 73–74

author, name of 28, 29, 30
authors, comparing Hughes to others
   75–76
autobiographies and biographical
   parallels 69–70, 134–141, 149–150
The Autobiography of Malcolm X
   (Malcolm X) 58

Baker, Houston A. 64
Baldwin, James 69
"Ballad of Booker T."
   attentive reading 120–122
   bibliography and online resources
   125
   compare and contrast essays 124–
   125
   form and genre 122–124
"Ballad of Booker T." sample topics
   Booker T. Washington in poetry
   124–125
   definitions of ballads 122–123
   philosophies of composition 123–
   124
   reassessing Booker T. Washington
   124
"Ballad of the Brown Girl" (Walker) 113
"Ballad of the Landlord" 34
ballads, defined 122–123
Baraka, Amiri. *See* Jones, Leroi
Berry, Faith 55, 70, 73, 74
The Big Sea
   attentive reading 134–137
   bibliography and online resources
   141

characters 139–140
history and context 140–141
themes 58, 137–139
The Big Sea sample topics
    black experiences in post–World
        War I Europe 140–141
    ceaseless movement and freedom
        from prejudices 138
    characterization of Hughes's father
        139
    characterization of specific
        luminaries of the Harlem
        Renaissance 139–140
    color lines and racial prejudices
        137–138
    the Harlem Renaissance 141
    illness and creativity 139
    racial identity and passing 137
    suspicion of religion 138–139
bildungsroman 174
biographical parallels. *See*
    autobiographies and biographical
    parallels
biographies, of Langston Hughes 54, 55
biracial characters 60, 61–62, 157–158
black culture 60
    see also African Americans
black is beautiful, theme of 58–59
black nationalism 51–52
*Black Struggle, Red Scare: Segregation
    and Anti-Communism in the South,
    1948–1668* (Wood) 65
block quotations 33–34
Bloom, Harold vii, 52
"The Blues I'm Playing"
    attentive reading 142–145
    bibliography and online resources
        151
    characters 146–147
    compare and contrast essays 73, 75,
        149–151
    form and genre 147–149
    themes 145–146
"The Blues I'm Playing" sample topics
    art and race relations 145–146
    biographical parallels 149–150
    black folk speech and art forms 148
    characterization through imagery
        147

female blues singers 146–147
form and structure of the story
    147–148
Guy de Maupassant and Langston
    Hughes 148–149
race relations in France and the
    United States 150
the ways of white folks and 145
white patronage, condescension,
    segregation, and hypocrisy
    150–151
blues music 52, 96–97, 173–174
body paragraphs 23–27
*Born in the U.S.A: The Myth of
    American in Popular Music from
    Colonial Times to the Present*
    (Scheurer) 72
brackets, quotations and 35
brainstorming 10
brass spittoons, in *Not Without
    Laughter* 175
"A Brown Girl Dead" (Cullen) 113

capitalizing, on Christ 118–119,
    182–183
ceaseless movement and freedom from
    prejudices 138
characterization through imagery 147
characters
    The Big Sea 139–140
    "The Blues I'm Playing" 146–147
    compare and contrast essays 9
    "Father and Son" 157–158
    Not Without Laughter 172
    philosophy and ideas 8
    symbols and 6
    Tambourines to Glory 183–184
    writing essays and 3–4, 60–62
children's literature 67–68
"Children's Rhymes" 72
citations and formatting 32–43
citizenship, struggle to achieve 105–106
civil rights 51–52, 62–63
clustering, preparing to write and 10
coherent paragraphs 25–27
common knowledge, plagiarism and 43
compare and contrast essays 8–9
    "Ballad of Booker T." 124–125
    "The Blues I'm Playing" 149–151

"The Negro Artist and the Racial
  Mountain" 129–133
"The Negro Speaks of Rivers" 89–91
Not Without Laughter 175–177
"Song for a Dark Girl" 112–113
Tambourines to Glory 188–190
"The Weary Blues" 97–99
writing essays and 73–76
composition, philosophies of 86–87,
  123–124
conclusions 30–32
contemporary style 62
continuities and discontinuities 74–75
continuity and change 156–157, 164
"Crossing" 71
Cullen, Countee 53, 70, 75, 76, 113,
  130–131
cultural context 1, 7–8

daily life 7
Death of a Salesman (Miller) 4
devils 183, 184
dialect and diction 187–188
Dickens, Charles 7
Dickinson, Emily 5
"Dixie, " history and meaning of 110–111
documenting sources 37–40, 40–43
double consciousness 101, 105
drama, genre and 4
dream deferred, the 71
"Dream Variation" 54, 58
Du Bois, W.E.B. 101, 105
"Dulce et decorum est" (Owen) 5
Dunbar, Paul Laurence 75

ellipses, quotations and 35–36
"Enter the New Negro" (Locke) 64
essays, by Hughes 59, 60, 126–133
essays, writing 1–2
  about Langston Hughes 51–56
  attentive reading 56–57
  bibliography and online resources
    76–81
  body paragraphs 23–27
  characters 60–62
  characters and 3–4
  choosing works to study and 56–57
  citations and formatting 32–43
  compare and contrast essays 8–9,
    71–72, 73–76

conclusions 30–32
form and genre 4–5, 68–70
history and context 7–8, 62–65
introductions 27–30
language, symbols, and imagery
  5–6, 71–72
outlines and 13–23
philosophy and ideas 8, 65–68
preparing to write 9–10
sample essay 43–50
themes 2, 57–60
thesis statements 10–13
works cited 50
Essie (*Tambourines to Glory*) 183–184
Europe, post–World War I era
  140–141
exploitation and abuse, poems against
  112–113

"Father and Son"
  attentive reading 152–155
  bibliography and online resources
    161
  characters 157–158
  form and genre 160–161
  history and context 158–160
  themes 155–157
"Father and Son" sample topics
  biracial characters 157–158
  continuity and change 156–157
  cruel parents 158
  dating the story through historical
    references 159–160
  fooling oneself and others 155–156
  form and structure of the story
    160–161
  lynching 158–159
  rebellion and independence 156
  retelling the Oedipus story 160
  the ways of whites and 155
fathers 172, 175–176
  see also parents
Fields of Wonder 71
figurative language 5
Fine Clothes to the Jew 74–75
first person narration 12–13
flat characters 3
focusing your topic 10
"Fog" (Sandburg) 5–6
folklore 53, 70, 190

folk speech and art forms 148, 166,
   187–188
fooling oneself and others 155–156
foreshadowing 187
formal outlines 14, 19–23
form and genre 4–5
   "Ballad of Booker T." 122–124
   "The Blues I'm Playing" 147–149
   "Father and Son" 160–161
   Langston Hughes and 52, 53
   Not Without Laughter 173–174
   "Slave on the Block" 165–167
   Tambourines to Glory 186
   writing essays and 68–70
form and structure of the story 160–
   161, 165–166
Frankenstein (Shelley) 8
free verse 68, 91
freewriting 10
Fried, A. 65

Gay, Peter 64
Gay Voices of the Harlem Renaissance
   (Schwarz) 67
gender roles 62
   see also women
"Goodbye Christ"
   attentive reading 115–116
   bibliography and online resources
      119
   history and context 116–117
   philosophy and ideas 117–119
"Goodbye Christ" sample topics
   1930s radicalism 116–117
   capitalizing on Christ 118–119
   Marxism and blacks 118
   McCarthyism and cold war America
      117
   skepticism toward organized religion
      117
gospel music 186
Great Migration, the 185

haiku 4
Harlem, *Tambourines to Glory* and
   188–189
Harlem Renaissance 51, 63–64, 75, 76,
   139–140
"Harlem Sweeties" 58, 59
Hawthorne, Nathaniel 6, 9

Heart of Darkness (Conrad) 24, 25, 27
Hester Prynne (*The Scarlet Letter*) 6
highlighting 10
historical references, dating stories
   through 159–160
history and context 7–8
   The Big Sea 140–141
   "Father and Son" 158–160
   "Goodbye Christ" 116–117
   Langston Hughes and 53, 55
   Not Without Laughter 172–173
   "Song for a Dark Girl" 110–111
   Tambourines to Glory 184–185
   "The Weary Blues" 96–97
   writing essays and 62–65
Hughes, Langston, writing about
   51–56
   attentive reading 56–57
   bibliography and online resources
      76–81
   Bloom on vii
   characters 60–62
   compare and contrast essays 73–76
   form and genre 68–70
   history and context 62–65
   language, symbols, and imagery
      71–72
   philosophy and ideas 65–68
   themes 57–60
Hull, Gloria T. 64
Hurston, Zora Neale 75
Hutcheon, Linda 72

"I, Too"
   attentive reading 101–103
   bibliography and online resources
      103–106
   optimism and 54
   philosophy and ideas 103–106
"I, Too" sample topics
   changes to the poem 104–105
   double consciousness 105
   racial equality 104
   the struggle to achieve full
      citizenship and 105–106
   Walt Whitman and Langston
      Hughes 103–104
"I, Too, Sing America" 75
identifying tags, quotations and 32–33
identity 53, 62, 137

"I Hear America Singing" (Whitman)
75
illness and creativity 139
imagery, characterization through 147
Infants of the Spring (Thurman) 54
informal outlines 14, 17–19
intertextuality 53
introductions 27–30
irony, recycled language and 72

Jimboy (*Not Without Laughter*) 172
Jim Crow's Last Stand 73–74
Jones, Leroi 53, 70, 75–76

language, symbols, and imagery 5–6
    Langston Hughes and 52
    "The Negro Artist and the Racial
        Mountain" 128–129
    Not Without Laughter 174–175
    Tambourines to Glory 187–188
    writing essays and 71–72
laundry lists, essays and 9
Laura (*Tambourines to Glory*)
    183–184
Leaves of Grass (Whitman) 76
Lewis, David Levering 63
literal images 5
literary modernism. *See* modernism
literature versus folklore 190
Locke, Alain 64
love, metaphors of 112
"Luani of the Jungles"
    Heart of Darkness (Conrad) and 24,
        25, 27
    outlines and 14–15, 17–23
    sample essay and 43–50
    thesis statements and 11, 12, 12–13
lynching 110, 158–159
lyric poetry 68, 69

manifesto, "The Negro Artist and the
    Racial Mountain" as 129–130
mapping, preparing to write and 10
Marxism 68, 118
Maupassant, Guy de 148–149, 166–167
McCarthyism 51, 65, 117
*McCarthyism: The Great American
    Red Scare: A Documentary History*
    (Fried) 65

McKay, Claude 75
metaphors 5–6
Miller, Arthur 4
*MLA Handbook for Writers of
    Research Papers* (Modern Language
    Association) 37, 38–39
modern art, black subjects in 165
modernism 64–65
Modernism and the Harlem Renaissance
    (Baker) 64
Modernism: The Lure of Heresy (Gay)
    64
Modern Language Association 37
Montage of a Dream Deferred 71,
    74–75
moon, the 71
"Mother to Son" 54
mountain, the 71
music 52, 96–97, 128, 173–174
musical styles, comparing and
    contrasting 74–75

names, of characters 3–4
narrative voice 8
narrators, characters and 3
nature 174–175
negritude 68, 87–88
"Negro" 53, 59, 90–91
"The Negro-Art Hokum" (Schuyler)
    132–133
"The Negro Artist and the Racial
    Mountain"
    attentive reading 126–128
    bibliography and online resources
        133
    compare and contrast essays 73,
        129–133
    language, symbols, and imagery 71,
        128–129
    themes 58, 60
"The Negro Artist and the Racial
    Mountain" sample topics
    American and African-American
        music 128
    changing duties of the artist
        131–132
    Hughes as prophet 128–129
    Langston Hughes and Countee
        Cullen 130–131

Langston Hughes and George S.
  Schuyler 132–133
manifesto for Hughes's poetry
  129–130
"The Negro Speaks of Rivers"
  attentive reading and 82–84
  bibliography and online resources
    91–93
  compare and contrast essays 89–91
  philosophy and ideas 86–89
  themes 53, 84–86
"The Negro Speaks of Rivers" sample
  topics
  black Egypt and Afrocentrism
    88–89
  different views of Africa 86
  free verse and democratic vistas 91
  global reach and negritude 87–88
  literal and figurative parents 85–86
  "Negro" and 90–91
  philosophies of composition 86–87
  present and past time 84–85
  visual and musical adaptations 89–90
1930s radicalism 116–117
notations, on the text 57
notetaking 10
Not Without Laughter
  attentive reading 168–172
  bibliography and online resources
    177–178
  characters 172
  compare and contrast essays
    175–177
  form and genre 173–174
  history and context 172–173
  language, symbols, and imagery
    174–175
Not Without Laughter sample topics
  African Americans in World War
    I 173
  bildungsroman 174
  black life in the early 20th century
    172–173
  black women and religion 175–176
  blues and gospel music 173–174
  brass spittoons 175
  Jimboy as fantasized father 172
  nature 174–175
  real and imagined fathers 175–176

small town versus big city 175
  Tempy and trying to be white 172
novels
  Not Without Laughter 168–178
  Tambourines to Glory 179–191

Oedipus story, retelling 160
online sources 43
Online Writing Lab (OWL) 37, 39
optimism 53–54
outlines 13–23
Owen, Wilfred 5

paragraphs, body 23–27
paraphrasing 35, 39–40
parenthetical citations 37–38, 39–40
parents
  The Big Sea 139
  "Father and Son" 158
  "The Negro Speaks of Rivers" 85–86
  Not Without Laughter 175–176
parody 72
patronage, condescension, and
  hypocrisy, white people and 150–
  151, 165
persona, optimistic 53–54
personal life, Langston Hughes and
  54–55
philosophy and ideas 2, 8
  "Goodbye Christ" 117–119
  "I, Too" 103–106
  "The Negro Speaks of Rivers" 86–89
  "Song for a Dark Girl" 111–112
  writing essays and 65–68
plagiarism 40–43
plays and novels, *Tambourines to Glory*
  186
"Poem" 54
poems
  "Ballad of Booker T." 120–125
  "Goodbye Christ" 115–119
  "I, Too" 101–106
  "Song for a Dark Girl" 107–114
  "The Negro Speaks of Rivers" 82–93
  "The Weary Blues" 94–100
poetry
  characters and 3
  form and 5
  genre and 4

quotations and 33
simplicity of 52–53
political beliefs 54–55, 65, 69, 116–117
popular culture 52, 53, 72
The Portable Harlem Renaissance
  (Lewis) 63
position, of thesis statements 12
prayer 111–112
prejudices, color lines and 137–138
preparing to write 9–10, 55–56
personal responses, characters and 3
primary sources, citations and
  formatting 32–38
"Proem." *See* "Negro"
pronouns, use of 26
prophet, Hughes as 128–129
protest poetry 69
psychology 53–55, 62, 66–67
punctuation, quotations and 33, 35–37

questions 11, 31
quotations 32–37, 41

race and racism
  "The Blues I'm Playing" 150
  history and context and 62–63
  "I, Too" and 104
  "Luani of the Jungles" 11, 12
  themes 53, 59
Rampersad, Arnold 41–43, 52
  biographies, of Langston Hughes
    55, 70
  different audiences and 74
  optimism and 54
  protest poetry 69
  sexuality and 66
reading, attentive 1
  "Ballad of Booker T." 120–122
  The Big Sea 134–137
  "The Blues I'm Playing" 142–145
  "Father and Son" 152–155
  "Goodbye Christ" 115–116
  "I, Too" 101–103
  "The Negro Artist and the Racial
    Mountain" 126–128
  "The Negro Speaks of Rivers" 82–84
  Not Without Laughter 168–172
  preparing to write and 10, 55–56
  "Slave on the Block" 162–163

"Song for a Dark Girl" 107–110
Tambourines to Glory 179–182
"The Weary Blues" 94–96
writing essays and 56–57
rebellion and independence 156
recycled language and irony 72
Red Scare, the. *See* McCarthyism
religion
  The Big Sea 138–139
  "Goodbye Christ" 117
  "Song for a Dark Girl" 111
  Tambourines to Glory 188
  "The Weary Blues" and 99
  women and 175–176, 189
repetition 26, 30–31
"A Rose for Emily" 2
round characters 3

sample essay 43–50
Sandburg, Carl 5–6
The Scarlet Letter (Hawthorne) 6
Scheurer, Timothy E. 72
Schuyler, George S. 132–133
secondary sources 38–40
secondary themes 2
sensory language 5
sermons, African-American 52
sexuality, Langston Hughes and
  66–67
Shakespeare in Harlem 73–74
Shelley, Mary 8
short stories
  "Father and Son" 152–161
  "Luani of the Jungles" 11
  "Slave on the Block" 162–167
  "The Blues I'm Playing" 142–151
similes 5
simplicity, Hughes's poetry and 52–53
skin tones 58, 59
"Slave on the Block"
  attentive reading 162–163
  bibliography and online resources
    167
  form and genre 165–167
  themes 164–165
"Slave on the Block" sample topics
  black subjects in modern art 165
  continuity and change 164
  folk speech and art forms 166

form and structure of the story
165–166
Guy de Maupassant and Langston
Hughes 166–167
ways of white folks and 164
white patronage, condescension,
segregation and hypocrisy 165
small town versus big city 175, 189–190
social classes 97
"Song for a Dark Girl"
attentive reading 107–110
bibliography and online resources
113–114
compare and contrast essays 112–
113
history and context 110–111
language, symbols, and imagery 72
philosophy and ideas 111–112
"Song for a Dark Girl" sample topics
history and meaning of "Dixie"
110–111
lynching 110
metaphors of love 112
poems about dead black girls 113
poems against exploitation and
abuse 112–113
religion and race 111
the use of prayer 111–112
sonnets 4
"The Sounds of Silence" (Tidwell) 67
sources, citations and formatting 31–43
stanzas, speakers, and literary effects 99
statements, thesis statements and 11
stereotyping 15, 16, 17–19
structure and form, of "The Blues I'm
Playing" 147–148
subtopics, outlines and 15–16
summarizing 30–31, 39–40, 41–42
symbolic language 52

Tambourines to Glory
attentive reading 179–182
bibliography and online resources
191
characters 183–184
compare and contrast essays 188–
190
folklore and 70
form and genre 186

history and context 184–185
language, symbols, and imagery
187–188
themes 182–183
Tambourines to Glory sample topics
black women and religion 189
brownskin angels and white devils
183
capitalizing on Christ 182–183
the devil figure 184
dialect and diction 187–188
Essie and Laura 183–184
foreshadowing 187
gospel music 186
the Great Migration 185
Harlem as mecca or ghetto 188–189
literature versus folklore 190
plays and novels 186
religious symbols 188
small town versus big city 189–190
urban black life in the 1950s
184–185
tangents, body paragraphs and 24–25
Tempy (Not Without Laughter) 172
terminology, consistent 15
themes 2
The Big Sea 137–139
"The Blues I'm Playing" 145–146
compare and contrast essays 9
"Father and Son" 155–157
Langston Hughes and 53
"The Negro Speaks of Rivers" 84–86
"Slave on the Block" 164–165
Tambourines to Glory 182–183
writing essays and 57–60
thesis statements 9, 10–13
attentive reading and 56
introductions and 27, 28, 29, 30
outlines and 13–14, 16, 17, 23
Thurman, Wallace 54
time, past and present 84–85
titles, of works 2, 4, 28, 29, 30
"To Negro Writers" 60, 71, 73
topics and strategies
"Ballad of Booker T." 122–125
The Big Sea 137–141
"The Blues I'm Playing" 145–151
"Father and Son" 155–161
"Goodbye Christ" 116–119

Langston Hughes and 57–76
"The Negro Artist and the Racial
    Mountain" 128–133
"The Negro Speaks of Rivers" 84–91
Not Without Laughter 172–177
"Slave on the Block" 164–167
"Song for a Dark Girl" 110–113
Tambourines to Glory 182–190
"The Weary Blues" 96–99
topic sentences, body paragraphs and
    24, 27
Tracy, Steven C. 52
transitional words and phrases 26, 27
Twain, Mark 8

unified paragraphs 23–25

vague outlines 13–15, 14–15
visual and musical adaptations, "The
    Negro Speaks of Rivers" 89–90

Walker, Alice 113
Washington, Booker T. 124–125
"The Weary Blues"
    attentive reading 94–96
    bibliography and online resources
        100
    compare and contrast essays 73, 75,
        97–99
    folklore and 70
    history and context 96–97

"The Weary Blues" sample topics
    black artists and 97–98
    class divisions among African
        Americans 97
    religious views 99
    stanzas, speakers, and literary effects
        99
    structure, history, and the meaning
        of the blues 96–97
When Harlem Was in Vogue (Lewis)
    63
white people
    "Father and Son" 155
    patronage, condescension, and
        hypocrisy 150–151, 165
    "Slave on the Block" 164
Whitfield, James M. 72
Whitman, Walt 75, 76, 103–104
women
    "black is beautiful" and 59
    blues singers and 146–147
    characters 60
    Harlem Renaissance and 64
    religion and 175–176, 189
    "Song for a Dark Girl" 113
Wood, Jeff 65
works, choosing 56–57
works cited 38, 40, 50
World War I 173

"Yet Do I Marvel" (Cullen) 75